Sweet Assorted

Other books by Jim Christy

POETRY
Palatine Cat (Four Humours Press, 1978)
The Sunnyside of the Deathhouse (Ekstasis, 1996)
Cavatinas for Long Nights (Ekstasis, 2001)
Marimba Forever (Guernica, 2010)

FICTION
Streethearts, novel (Simon & Pierre, 1981)
Traveling Light, stories (Simon & Pierre, 1982)
Shanghai Alley, novel (Ekstasis, 1997)
Junkman, stories (Ekstasis, 1998)
Princess and Gore (Ekstasis, 2000)
Terminal Avenue, novel (Ekstasis, 2002)
Tight Like That, stories (Anvil, 2003)
The Redemption of Anna Dupree, novel (Ekstasis, 2005)
Nine O'Clock Gun, novel (Ekstasis, 2008)
Real Gone, novella (Quattro Books, 2010)

BIOGRAPHY
The Price of Power: A Biography of Charles Bedaux (Doubleday, 1983)
The BUK Book, Musings on Charles Bukowski (ECW, 1997)
The Long Slow Death of Jack Kerouac (ECW, 1998)
Scalawags: Rogues, Roustabouts, Wags & Scamps
—Brazen Ne'er-Do-Wells Through the Ages (Anvil, 2008)

TRAVEL
Rough Road to the North (Doubleday, 1980)
Letter from the Khyber Pass (D&M, 1992)
Between the Meridians (Ekstasis, 1999)

ESSAYS
Beyond the Spectacle (Aline Press, 1973)

NON-FICTION
Flesh and Blood: A Journey into the Heart of Boxing (D&M, 1990)
Strange Sites: Uncommon Homes & Gardens of the Pacific Northwest (Harbour, 1995)

Sweet Assorted

121 TAKES FROM A TIN BOX

BY JIM CHRISTY

Anvil Press | 2012

Copyright © 2012 by Jim Christy

Anvil Press Publishers Inc.
P.O. Box 3008, Main Post Office
Vancouver, B.C. V6B 3X5 Canada
www.anvilpress.com

All rights reserved. No part of this book may be reproduced by any means without the prior written permission of the publisher, with the exception of brief passages in reviews. Any request for photocopying or other reprographic copying of any part of this book must be directed in writing to Access Copyright: The Canadian Copyright Licensing Agency, One Yonge Street, Suite 800, Toronto, ON., Canada, M5E 1E5.

Library and Archives Canada Cataloguing in Publication

Christy, Jim, 1945-
Sweet assorted : 121 takes from a tin box / Jim Christy.

ISBN 978-1-927380-05-5

1. Christy, Jim, 1945-. 2. Files (Records)--Anecdotes.
3. Clippings (Books, newspapers, etc.)--Anecdotes. 4. Souvenirs (Keepsakes)--Anecdotes. 5. Authors, Canadian (English)--Biography. I. Title.

PS8555.H74Z475 2012   C818'.5409   C2012-905492-5

Book design: Derek von Essen

Represented in Canada by the Literary Press Group.

Distributed in Canada by the University of Toronto Press
and in the U.S. by Small Press Distribution (SPD).

The publisher gratefully acknowledges the financial assistance of the Canada Council for the Arts, the Canada Book Fund, and the Province of British Columbia through the B.C. Arts Council and the Book Publishing Tax Credit.

Printed and bound in Canada.

TABLE OF CONTENTS

Preface ...7

The Takes ...9

About the Author ...192

PREFACE

For nearly forty years I've had this metal Peek Frean's box into which I've tossed items randomly, willy-nilly and with neither rhyme nor reason. There has been absolutely no system to it. Maybe I thought, "I'll pay more attention to this later," or perhaps, "I've got to check that one out some day…," "Give it the attention it deserves…," "Since there's no other place to put this old razor…" I am not a person with an organized file system or, for that matter, a disorganized file system, so into the box it went. There are other boxes, but none of them as curious as my Sweet Assorted box.

One evening in 1974, I answered an ad in the paper announcing an old yellow pickup truck for sale. I went to see the thing on Lonsdale Avenue, and the seller and I kept sneaking curious glances at each other. Turns out it was David Duplain, whom I had met and hung out with four years earlier in Amsterdam. One particular night, we were to grab a meal and a couple of drinks, but Duplain left me a note saying he had to cancel because he'd met a woman; he was sure I'd understand. I did. I never saw or heard from him again until I answered the ad.

Turns out that he married that woman he met in Amsterdam. She was from Geneva and followed him to Canada. When he started his company, he called it Geneva Gardens.

I didn't buy the truck but I started working for David Duplain and stayed working for him three or four days a week for five years.

For a couple of seasons, Geneva Gardens had a contract to maintain hydro properties throughout the city. There was a hydro station on O'Connor Drive in East York, and one day, after finishing the property, I noticed a shiny cream-yellow and royal-blue box in an adjacent vacant lot. I went and retrieved it. Made of tin, it would have offered a selection of cookies made by Peek Frean's, officially Peek, Frean & Co., Ltd., London, S.E. 16, England; the selection was called Sweet Assorted. The company had a plant in the vicinity of the hydro station.

I took the box home, and chance began to do its work. The box has filled up, and the inside reminds me of barnacles on the hull of an old boat. It is no longer shiny; it may have gathered some rust but no moss. It has moved around frequently, sat on the floor, on a table, under a table, in a garage and in the trunk of a 1978 Buick out in a field. At times I haven't had any idea where it was; often, for months or years, I never gave it a thought. Then one day a few months ago, I was wondering about the box and wishing I had it with me. I sure would like to see it again and rifle through its contents. Read again about the man who'd been in bed for forty years—whatever happened to him?—and those women on that weird agricultural apparatus, gliding down low over the fields—what were they picking? Artichokes, Brussels sprouts? And lo and behold, I looked across the room, and on the top shelf of a deep cabinet, behind some books, there it was.

What was the first thing I tossed into the box? I've often wondered but couldn't, and can't, remember. What if at the moment the first item found its new home, I had said to myself, "That's number one. You're going to be filling that box for forty years. What will be in Sweet Assorted all those decades later when you take inventory?" (Quite frankly, I couldn't have entertained such a question, because I wouldn't have been able to get past the notion of living another forty years. And if I had known I was going to do what I've done, I never would have done it.)

Going through the box, taking inventory, has meant one discovery after another. I have felt like a prospector but I have not "salted" my claim. Nothing has been added for the purpose of making the contents "more interesting." I have had, unfortunately, to delete a few items in order to avoid interfering with anyone's privacy.

When I began rifling through the box this time, I realized there was a story behind every item, except maybe the cow with the head of a rooster and the pig with two rear ends.

TAKE 1

BOARDING PASS FOR FLIGHT 994/964, SMITHERS, B.C., TO VANCOUVER, B.C., 28 NOVEMBER 1994

I was in the Yukon and got a ride on a lumber truck from a woodlot near Watson Lake to Smithers with a man who frequently made this same run. He told me that every winter he went to work in Russia for a couple of months, and when his contract was done, he spent ten days at a resort on the Dead Sea. The waters there were good for his psoriasis. It was a great trip down Highway 97 past Mount Bedaux and Fern Lake. The driver told stories about the hermits that lived in the forest. I remember one about the fellow who robbed the general store/gas station whenever he got the notion. This was inconvenient for all concerned, because somebody would have to be dispatched to go and retrieve whatever he'd stolen—usually potato chips and fishing gear. The man sincerely believed he was a master thief (sort of a Manolesco or Arsène Lupin) and wouldn't get caught in his far-north hideaway.

This story reminded me of another one, about this guy in Dawson City—I think he was nineteen or twenty—who lived with his parents in a double-wide. A few times each year, he'd rob the Imperial Bank of Commerce, Robert Service's old bank. One of the bank staff would telephone the Mounties, who'd groan and say, "Don't tell me he did it again!" They, in turn, went and knocked on the door of the trailer, whereupon one or both parents would groan and say, "Don't tell me he did it again!" A Mountie always found the kid in his room and the money in canvas bags under the bed. The kid would be taken down to the office and given a good talking-to whenever anyone got around to it. He'd be told to go home, unless it was winter, in which case he'd be driven back to the trailer.

I was surprised that the truck driver knew nothing of Ralph Edwards, the legendary "Crusoe of Lonesome Lake," who had homesteaded way back in the bush at a place in the southern part of what is now Tweedsmuir Provincial Park. For a time, he was the ultimate hermit, although he hadn't always been. Edwards was born in North Carolina but raised by missionary parents in the Himalayas in India. Later he went to school in Massachusetts before pursuing a drifter's life. He wound up in British Columbia on a construction crew and claimed land to homestead.

He spent seven years alone, save for whomever he encountered when he set off for supplies, which entailed a four-day trip with a pack mule when conditions were ideal. Edwards fished, hunted and farmed, making everything he used, including his tools. He left for four years to serve in the army in France in the First World War. When he returned, he had a wife. They raised a family back in the woods and had no modern conveniences, except for a single light bulb that worked on power generated by a stream near the house. At age sixty-two, he left the homestead to get his pilot's licence, having studied for years and built his own plane. In 1965, he and his wife separated, and at the age of seventy, Edwards left the bush to live in Prince Rupert and work as a commercial fisherman. He died there at age seventy-seven.

But the Crusoe tag was applied to him by people who must not have read Mr. Defoe's book. A great book, but its subject had advantages not available to Ralph Edwards. Robinson, readers will recall, was the only survivor of a shipwreck and he was able to walk through a shallow stream from land to the ship and cart off its contents. So in the beginning, Crusoe had a leg up. Edwards, by contrast, made everything, including wooden ball bearings for his machinery.

TAKE 2

ST. AUGUSTINE ALLIGATOR FARM POSTCARD; PHOTO OF '58 CADILLAC BY SIGN FOR REAL LIFE RANCH; PLUS MUELLER CARD

The front of the postcard, relic of an age of insulting stereotypes, features what your good old-time rednecks—"conchs" (conks) in North Florida—referred to as your good old-time darkie sitting on the back of an alligator and smiling, like "Yassuh, eba thang aw right wid de worl." There are several other alligators visible, plus sand and palm fronds. The photo is an old one, coloured in the darkroom. The legend reads, "Taking it Easy in Florida at the St. Augustine Alligator and Ostrich Farm." The place had ceased to have ostriches by the '70s, and the man's lips are a preternatural red.

The back of the card bears a message addressed to "Jim/Mary-Anne" at Woodlawn Avenue in Vancouver. Although the card originated at St. Augustine, it was mailed on "10/6/85" at Vancouver. It reads:

Dear Jim + Mary-Anne
Summertime and the living is easy. Or so the song says.
I bought a fifth of scotch last night to celebrate the return
of warm wind. Let's get together soon and discuss meteorological
phenomena. Like the way the sun goes down in St. Augustine.

Kerry

The card is from a Vancouver journalist named Kerry Banks. Although we've drifted apart and haven't seen each other for twenty years, Kerry and I were fairly good friends for a time. He had an interest in sports and liked to travel. Kerry was going down to Florida, and I told him that by all means he must stop in St. Augustine. I told him about the Spanish architecture, the mix of peoples, the fact that the old town was free of the franchise monoculture that marred the coastal areas of the rest of the state.

St. Augustine has a curious history, being the oldest continuously inhabited settlement in the United States, originally founded by Spaniards from Minorca. There were a couple of buildings still standing that were built in the late 1600s. Two centuries later, the U.S. government shipped Geronimo to its prison in St. Augustine. The local archivist, learning that I had spent considerable time in the Yukon, informed me that the Lady Known As Lou (in the words of Robert Service) had retired to St. Augustine and built a mansion on San Marco Avenue. Henry Flagler put up a grand hotel in St. Augustine, but when the Florida boom headed south, the place stood vacant until becoming a college named for its builder. The former hotel ballroom still possessed a huge chandelier, the installation of which had been supervised by Mister Tiffany himself.

So Kerry had stopped there for a few days and sent us this card upon his return to Vancouver.

The first time I saw St. Augustine was in 1965 when I was drifting around the country with a friend. We had stopped at the town square—still known by white locals as the old slave market—and marvelled at the beauty of the place. It was so refreshingly un-American. We were staring at the elaborate Episcopal church when a very attractive dark-skinned and black-haired, teenaged girl walked by.

"Did you notice that young lady, brother?" Val asked.

"I certainly did."

"Have you ever seen the like?" he drawled.

"Can't say that I have."

Ten years later, having grown sick and tired of Toronto winters, I began to spend all or parts of those dreary months in St. Augustine. When I met Mary Anne during my second extended stay, I was convinced—or convinced myself—that she had been the very same sixteen-year-old girl that Val and I had seen all those years before. We would be together and apart for several years.

So what does all this have to do with Kerry's postcard from the Alligator Farm and the photo of the '58 Cadillac before the "Real Life Ranch"?

Well, I'll tell you.

I came to know the main man at the Alligator Farm. Like the fellow on the front of the card, he was black, but he was no darkie. His name was Chris, and when I first met him, he had just opened a joint called the Gator Club. That would have been in 1977. The clientele was all black almost all the time. Occasionally I stopped in at the Gator Club. I'm white. Integration had been legislated a decade and a half or so earlier but it didn't mean much in the South. Even in St. Augustine, which was sophisticated compared to—for instance—nearby Palatka to the west, no black would have dreamed of trying to buy a drink in any bar that wasn't exclusively black.

I was permitted to go in there but I didn't make a habit of it. Chris was friendly, most of the people ignored me and several wanted to kill me. The truth of that last part was affirmed one night when some of the patrons almost did. Anyway, Mary Anne, with her black eyes and black hair and dark skin, could pass as some kind of mixed blood, like Jennifer Beals in *Devil in a Blue Dress*; or as a Fijian, maybe; or a native of the Maldives. She asked Chris for a job and worked at the Gator Club a couple of nights a week.

One afternoon I was driving around St. Augustine Beach, just across the Bridge of Lions from the centre of town, when I spied, parked by the side of a service station, a three-toned (green, white and gold) 1958 Cadillac four-door hardtop with a For Sale sign on the windshield. It was love at first sight.

I stopped to enquire, and the old redneck owner was asking about a quarter of what I figured it was worth. I told him I wanted it, and he ran his big hands lovingly along the front fender. He reminded me of the old rodeo star and cowboy actor Ben Johnson. He said, "Boy, I will sell you this car but you got to promise me one thing."

"What's that?"

"Should you ever want to sell her, you won't sell her to no nigger."

"Okay."

"No, you got to promise."

"I promise."

"Well, okay, then."

I had a ball driving that car around the countryside. One time I drove it to Toronto and left it in a garage on Brunswick Avenue while I went to the Yukon. Upon my return, the car looked so forlorn and out of place, its tail fins sticking out of the garage and covered with snow. It was January. I packed her up and headed south. I had filled a box with books and put it in the trunk. The U.S. border guards were mystified by this.

"Why do you have all those books?"

"I'm going to read them."

"You are?"

"Yes."

"You sure?"

"Well, I'm going to try."

"Why?" and so on.

I liked St. Augustine very much, met some good people and had plenty of fine times. I worked for a few weeks parking cars at the

Ripley's Believe It or Not Museum that was down the street from my small apartment over a garage on Rhode Avenue. Across from my apartment was another apartment I had inquired about, only to be told it wasn't available. I learned that it hadn't been available for several years. It seems that the owner of the house had been so unwise as to rent the apartment to a mixed couple: black man, white woman. The pair was continually harassed until finally the man was kicked to death in a parking lot. The local white supremacists were still punishing the house owner all these years later, threatening her should she try to rent to anyone, even white people.

The town was filled with rednecks, boat people, permanent refugees, and tourists. Sometimes the first two categories melded. If you belonged to either of the second two categories and were from up north, you had to live in a kind of isolation. I was spared that, being Canadian. After all, Canada (or Great Britain) had supported the South in the War Between the States. Plus, I had, eventually, a local lady friend and a Cadillac with Florida plates.

There were some interesting refugees, one being an aristocratic though gently daft man from central New Jersey called Merrill Morris. He came from old money and, thanks to good looks and a mellifluous voice, had been one of the very first television anchor men. He was also a pretty fair jazz drummer. Merrill had fallen on bad times as the result of an automobile accident fifteen years earlier, in which he rolled his MG convertible; it was the resultant head injuries that had left him gently daft. I had thought he was a poor man, living on a paltry disability cheque until I saw on his dresser top, three uncashed cheques from a brokerage firm in New York.

"Hey, Merrill. Why don't you cash these so you can buy yourself a decent dinner?"

He looked at me like that was a novel idea, and why hadn't he thought of it.

Another interesting refugee had come all the way from Vienna via a concentration camp. He had a nook in an old Spanish building across the road from Flagler College. Anton Mueller. He sold books and prints. I'd visit for a couple of hours, listening to him talk of Vienna and café society. Of the camps, he wouldn't speak.

It was people like Anton and Merrill who made the place enjoyable. The locals looked at me askance because I associated with such people and didn't use the N-word in every other sentence.

In 1981 I knew I'd soon be moving to Vancouver, and that was a little too far away to maintain my connection with St. Augustine. Chris had asked me about the car every time I saw him over the past three years. Finally, he said, "Mary Anne tells me you're not coming back to town and you have to get rid of the Cadillac. Well, man, you got a buyer, you know that."

"I can't sell it to you, Chris."

"Why not? I'll pay your price."

"Well, you see, I made a promise to the peckerwood sold me the short."

"Yeah, what was the promise?"

"I promised him that if I ever sold the car I wouldn't sell it to a 'nigger,' and I'm quoting."

He gave me the flat look.

"I didn't think you were like the rest of them."

"I'm not. But I'm a man of my word."

"Shit."

"So I'm not going to sell it to you, Chris. I'm going to give it to you."

And I handed him the keys.

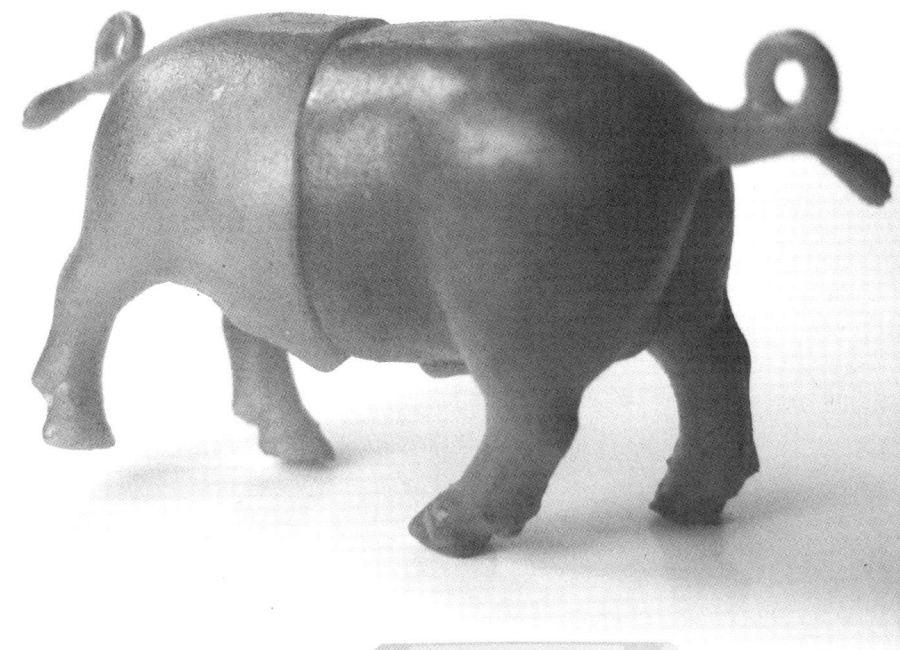

TAKE 3

A PLASTIC PIG WITH TWO HIND PARTS BUT NO HEAD—OR HEADS

Somewhere along the line, I glued or melted together the back ends of these poor pigs. Once upon a time, I had a cow with the neck and head of a duck or a chicken in this box but I used it in an art piece.

TAKE 4

PHOTOGRAPH, BAR EL GALEÓN, AT EL PROGRESO, YUCATAN, MEXICO

El Progresso is a half-hour ride by local bus from Mérida. The beach, in the mid-'90s, was always deserted or nearly so, and the prices were less than half those of the city. The sands were white, but the water was brown, being on the Atlantic side of the country. It's a tough oil town, and El Galeón was not for gringos. It was the kind of place I'd expect to see Álvaro Mutis's hero Maqroll, the *gaviero*. But Maqroll is not a gringo—or is he? No one knows. Maqroll tells stories long into the night in bars like El Galeón, but you never learn his nationality. I once asked Mutis about him, but Mutis only smiled.

Mutis, a winner of the Cervantes Prize, is in his eighties now and is often considered to be the second-best writer in the Spanish language, his friend Gabriel García Márquez, being the first. Personally, I believe the order should be reversed.

Mutis's protagonist—I think of him as a hero—gets involved in one impossible situation after another, and nothing ever works out to his advantage. The reader knows it will turn out badly and gets the sense that Maqroll does too but can't help himself. There is something noble in his grand misadventures.

The first time I was ever in El Progreso, I'd been following the route of the 1839–40 Walker-Caddy expedition from Belize City across the Petén of Guatemala, down the river to Tabasco State and on to Palenque in Chiapas.

The great Mayan ceremonial site of Palenque was first seen by outsiders in the mid-18th century. All sorts of weird stories and lurid illustrations were brought out of the jungle over the years by mostly eccentric explorers, chief among these being Comte Jean de Waldeck, an artist, adventurer and rogue. Waldeck lived to be 100 years old. (Dying of a heart attack while sitting at an outdoor café in Paris, he turned to watch a pretty girl walk by.) People like Waldeck were considered unreliable, so the Special Ambassador to Central America, John Lloyd Stephens, who happened to be an antiquarian, decided to find Palenque and look it over. To document the site, Stephens brought along the artist Frederick Catherwood.

The British government learned of the forthcoming expedition and, worried that there might be some commercial advantages to be had from the journey, it hastily put together its own team. The leader was a sort of Belize busybody named Patrick Walker, and his artist was a captain of the Royal Canadian Engineers, John Herbert Caddy. Central American newspapers touted the "Race to Palenque." The participants didn't see it that way, but for the record, Walker and Caddy got there first.

About the journey, Walker produced a dry report illustrated by Caddy that vanished into the archives of the British Foreign Office. Stephens, however, wrote the great work of Central American exploration, *Incidents of Travel in Central America, Chiapas and Yucatan*, and included Catherwood's drawings, which have become ubiquitous to Central American antiquities.

The Walker-Caddy story would have ended with Walker's report, had not an employee of the Royal Ontario Museum come across Caddy's journal of the trip, which contained some of his rough sketches. David Pendergast published a book about the expedition with the University of Oklahoma Press, and I came across it in a curio shop in Antiqua Guatemala. Caddy was quite a fellow, remarkably free of the prejudices of his time, with a sharp eye and a deft pen. His journal is exceptional for a quality lacking in almost all books of exploration and adventure: a sense of humour. Were there any justice—which there isn't, of course—it would be he and not Catherwood who would be famous.

Caddy eventually returned to Canada, where he taught painting in Hamilton, helped lay out plans for the City of London and retired to roam around the countryside painting. You can pick up one of his paintings for $1,500.

I had my own adventures on my travels in the region and was in much need of the rest and relaxation I hoped to get in El Progreso, which is why I ventured a visit to El Galeón.

I got out alive.

(Note the dark leg and white high-heel shoe visible below the swinging doors.)

TAKE 5

YELLOW EXTRA VOUCHER

Everybody in Vancouver in the '80s worked in films in one capacity or another. I did a lot of extra work and had a few speaking parts. I rode a hook on a crane across the water from a barge to a wharf, strangled a doctor and was in an episode of a TV show that featured Bette Davis, sold bagels in the Depression, spoke three lines in Russian and sang in a convict choir, but not in the same film.

This voucher is for something called *Top of the Hill*, a Cannell production. I have absolutely no memory of this, don't know what *Top of the Hill* was, a TV series, TV movie or regular feature. I'm not interested in looking it up, either.

The best thing about being in all those productions was the people I encountered; the worst thing was the people too. The other silent-on-cameras—people who had no lines but were featured in close-ups or did a particular bit of business while the cameras were on them, sort of glorified extras—were interesting, and some of the stars were engaging and unpretentious. Ed Asner, for instance. We talked about Nicaragua. Scatman Crothers was good company. The worst people I met were mid-level principals, followed closely by the young kids hustling their way to the top. The top of what? They'd do anything—*anything*— to get a close-up. The old notion of the casting couch is laughably quaint where these fools are concerned.

TAKE 6

TWO BREAKFAST COUPONS, HOTEL WINA, KUTA BEACH, BALI

The hotel was filled with French package-tourists. The ladies wore a lot of makeup, and the men hit the beach in thong bikinis. And these were men of middle or more than middle age. We stayed at Hotel Wina for two days, the 16th and 17th of January. The year was 2001.

Kuta itself catered to young Australians, each of whom seemed to have a tattoo. During the day, they worked on their skin cancer, drank and went bungee jumping. At night, they drank at discos like the one that was bombed the next year.

We were glad to get out of there and see the rest of the island.

In Bali, I stopped at the Kuta Beach Hotel Resort and was just looking around when a woman stepped from behind the reception desk and started telling me about the founding of the hotel by a man called Robert Koke and a woman "who had a whole bunch of names and was later famous on the radio during the War."

This "rang a bell," as they say, and later I thought about it as I lay on the beach at Lovina on the other side of the island, an area much more conducive to contemplation than busy, overcrowded Kuta. Why, I asked myself, was this bit about a lady on the radio who had many names so familiar? I was wading in the warm, shallow waters one day, my mind a complete and peaceful blank, when it came to me. Ten years earlier, I was in Australia and paid a visit to the film commission in Sydney. There was an old lady there who kept interrupting the conversation I was trying to have with an official, going on about her life: "I did this," she said, "I did that... Noel Coward told me...Chaplin said...My friend Suharto..." *[Note: Though she might have said "Sukarno."]* When she left, the man said, "She's quite a character, that old gal. Used to be known as Surabaya Sue and broadcast for the guerillas during the battle for the independence of Indonesia; before that, the Japanese put her in prison. She put up a hotel, was an artist, all sorts of things. If we could just separate truth from fiction, we'd do a film about her."

"Why not do the film about just that: what's true, what's not?"

Indeed, it was the infamous Surabaya Sue I had met. She was also known as Mrs. Manx, Muriel Pearson, Vannen Walker, Miss Tenchery, Miss Daventry and K'tut Tantri.

She was perhaps born on the Isle of Man in 1898; it is known that she pursued the life of a bohemian artist in San Francisco in the '30s, arriving in Bali at the end of that decade. She did build a hotel, resist the Japanese, become involved with the Indonesian independence movement, become a Department of Information official; she travelled the world, was active in the trade union movement in Australia, and died in that country in 1997, age ninety-nine. She left her estate to the poor children of Indonesia.

As is usually the case with people, especially women, who have lived extraordinary lives, many of her exploits are questioned.

TAKE 7

POSTCARD WITH PICTURE OF MISS SWEDEN

Everyone called her Miss Sweden. She was friendly and talkative but not given to reminiscing. She was pleasantly pudgy, wore harem pants, loads of jewelry, veils, leis and a halter top emblazoned with the legend "Sweden Social Democrat." Her usual beat was Bloor Street between Spadina and Bathurst, where I saw her throughout the '70s and until I moved west in December 1981.

The postcard is from my good friend Phil Surguy (1941–2008). Phil was interested in everything. We met at a party in 1976, although for the previous six months we had nodded to each other over breakfast at a restaurant on Spadina, just south of Bloor on the west side.

Phil was a dedicated *flâneur*. I remember fondly our long walks around the city. I had to keep my distance from him. Phil was a big guy, and the way he walked reminded me of some huge four-door sedan with faulty springs, like the one the Joads drove to California with trunks sliding around the roof, hubcaps popping off, destined for the ditches. His feet kicked out and to the sides and his arms flailed around like he was trying to escape his invisible captors. He walked fast but stopped often and abruptly to read bills posted on walls and telephone poles. He seemed to know obscure details about every street we explored and he would stop and talk to anyone. Naturally, he was friendly with Miss Sweden.

On the other side of the postcard, he wrote "Here is the contents of P.O. Box 124, as of Dec. 21 – c. 1:P.M. ..." (I was probably in St. Augustine.) "Things are more or less the same around here: cold; almost making a living; pecking away at the novel. Learned a new (to me) word: toxophilite; it means a lover of archery.

"There seems to be a word for everything. Enjoyed your review of the Morris-Jones book in last Sat's *Globe*. Reading from *Here to E.* when I was 15 was the first time I ever imagined being a writer—a vivid experience, though not quite as overwhelming as T. Wolfe's mystic call to J. Jones. I trust the -----." The rest of the line is smudged. Below his signature is an arrow and "card #2." But I don't have card #2.

In the photograph, Miss Sweden is standing in front of a store window that displays a plastic clown punching bag, a baseball, a glove, cap and several pool balls. There is also a bug-eyed plastic green-coloured creature partially obscured by the plinth, up against which leans the clown punching bag. Miss Sweden has her head bent to the left, her left hand holds a gaudy green purse, and her right hand is at her side but bent backward: it's as if she's about to break into some old Swedish folk dance.

In the window parallel to her extended right forearm is the reflection of two men in sport coats, caught in midstride. The light seems to be autumn light, but Miss Sweden has her shoulders bare as always.

I wonder what happened to her. I've asked the people I know who remember her, just as we used to ask each other about her history. But no one seems to know what happened to her, just as we never knew what her story was.

The photograph was produced by Coach House Post Card Printing Co., and I'm guessing that was a division of Coach House Press. There is a blemish on the bottom left-hand corner of the card where the photographer's name appears to be Peter Rowe (but it could be Rowen or a variation). I hope they paid her something for the use of her image. I looked into that, but nobody remembers.

TAKE 8

SKETCH BY ME OF A TALL FELLOW DRESSED IN RED PANTS AND SHIRT WITH A BLACK BELT

He has purple lips, orange skin and green hair, and occupies the back of a receipt, dated 08-20-06, for $9.39, from Gwartzman's Art Supplies, Spadina Avenue, Toronto. I don't remember anything about the sketch. I like to think it is an accurate portrait of someone I saw walking by or waiting for the Spadina streetcar. Maybe it was a Progressive-Conservative Party politician who wanted to cut the feeble pension cheque I was due to start receiving in a few years.

TAKE 9

STATEMENT OF EARNINGS, FROM L.H. PERCY & COMPANY, 1605 SUMMER STREET, PHILADELPHIA 3, PA., FOR WEEK ENDING AUGUST 22, 1966.

I can't believe I've kept this statement on creamy off-white paper for forty-some years. (Well, yes, I can, because I've kept the rest of this box's contents.) I had a thousand jobs before moving to Canada in 1968. Most of those jobs involved manual labour. This one, with L.H. Percy, an advertising and public relations company, was an exception. I vaguely remember Mr. Percy himself: he had salt-and-pepper hair and a moustache, and reminded me of Louis Calhern who played "White Russians" in Paris and Marilyn Monroe's sugar daddy in *Asphalt Jungle*.

I don't remember applying for the job, but making my rounds is still very clear. It was an easy job, and I got to wear all the sharp threads I retained from the job I was doing immediately before this one. (All I'll say about that activity is that there were no gangsters at L.H. Percy.) I had also enrolled in college at midterm in order not to be classified 1-A with the draft board.

So there I was, going to class sometimes and working sometimes. What I did was solicit ads for a yearbook for the Volunteer Fire Companies of Chester County, Pennsylvania. The money that I gathered was split between the companies and L.H. Percy. The firemen got forty percent, Percy got sixty percent, and I got half of that. It's not as if the advertisers forked over the dough because of any smooth spiel on my part; it's more like they paid out of guilt. The yearbook would note the donors, and it wouldn't look so good if the local car dealer hadn't paid up. Also, what if the car dealership caught on fire?

That particular week, I sold ads ranging in cost from $5 to $60. It's curious that savings-and-loan associations and investment companies took the $5 ads and businesses like lumberyards and brickyards the $60 ads. My customers included American Lacquer Solvents, Boiler Engineering and Supply Company, Coatesville Plumbing and Ingelside Lanes.

That week I brought in $615 in cheques and $70 in cash. Of the $685, my thirty percent came to $205.50. Not bad for fifteen hours one week in 1966.

I finished the firefighter yearbook and was offered an architect's book as my next project. The ads would be much more expensive and I would naturally make much more money. Mr. Percy told me, however, that I'd have to dress more conservatively and keep my hair cut short. I didn't want anyone telling me how to dress; as well, my political ideas were becoming more radical. I told Mr. Percy I couldn't do it. He shook his head and shrugged.

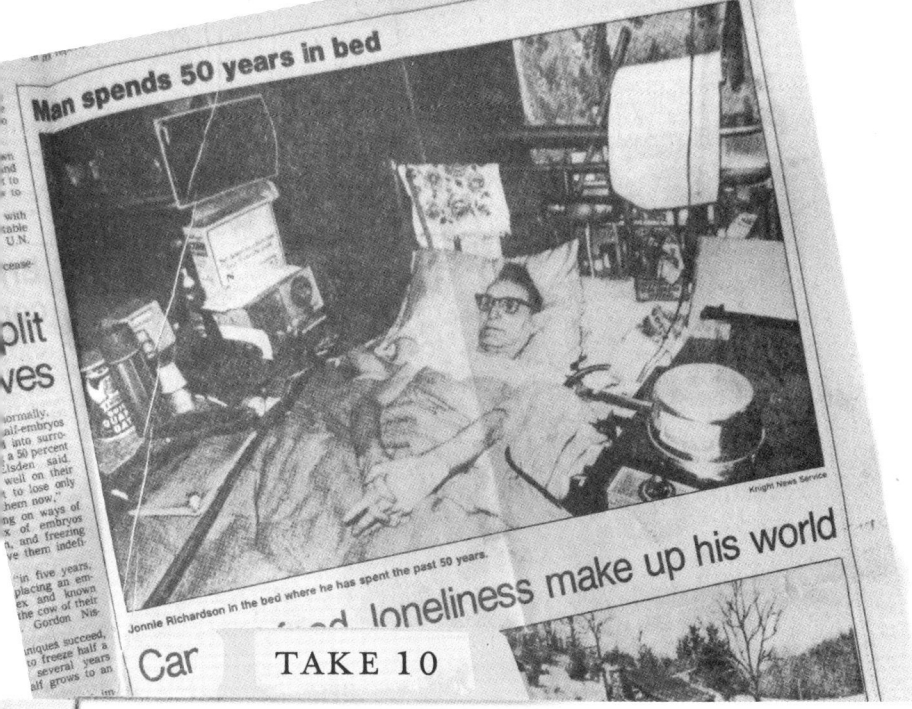

NEWSPAPER STORY HEADED "MAN SPENDS 50 YEARS IN BED"

There are two photographs accompanying the piece. One shows a cabin in the hills; the other, a man lying in bed with only his head, arms and folded hands visible. He is wearing black-framed glasses, and the way his hair stands up calls to mind a semi-Mohawk. Around the man are arranged a hot plate, a lamp, a radio, a box of Quaker Oats and the like.

I'm pretty sure the clipping is from the *Seattle Times* and although it is not dated, it must be from 1982. A fragment of a story under "Northwest" on the back of the clipping mentions an investigation in Snohomish County. Another story mentions that United States President Andrew Jackson had trouble with the Falkland Islands "151 years ago" in 1831. Under "Nation" is the teaser, "At the age of 16, Jonnie Richardson climbed into a big double bed in his parents' isolated mountain shack to rest. Fifty years later, he is still resting."

So here is the entire page-one story:

Canned food, loneliness make up his world

Laurel Springs, N.C.—Fifty years ago, when he was 16 years old, Jonnie Richardson went to bed and never got up again. A youth who helped his family eke out a bare living on their mountainous Ashe County farm, he was bothered by occasional illness.

Doctors couldn't pinpoint the trouble. Finally, one decided that most of his illness originated with a goiter in his neck and a heart that beat too fast.

When they couldn't cure him, Jonnie Richardson took matters into his own hands. "I went to bed in 1932," he said. "I haven't raised up since 1942 and I haven't turned over since 1960."

Not much that has since happened outside the walls of the weather-beaten, 95-year-old house has touched him. Through World War II, the Vietnam War, assassinations and international crises, 66-year-old Jonnie Richardson has lain in bed, looking out the windows of the decaying old house, watching deer feeding in the pasture, studying his beloved mountains.

His parents, who cared for him into their 80s, died years ago.

They lie in the little family cemetery on the hill above the house. A couple of surviving sisters live a few hollows away, but he seldom sees them. They are old and do not drive, and travel in this rugged land is not easy.

Thank God for Bessie. His sister, Bessie Richardson. Sixty-nine now, living a quarter-mile or so away. Handicapped by a hip broken last April, leaning heavily on a cane, she still makes the painful way across the hill almost daily to care for her brother. When snow isolates him, a couple of neighbors take turns coming by to stoke the small wood stove that heats the uninsulated room. They put the boxes of cereal and the cans of food on which Jonnie lives where he can reach them.

When you are bedridden and living on $159.30 a month Social Security, survival isn't easy. Jonnie Richardson copes. Drinking water flows through a hose from a spring 700 feet away.
Bessie rigged a second hose to pipe water into a Clorox bottle basin beside Richardson's bed. Another hose carries away urine. Plastic bags take care of other bodily functions.
He warms his food in a toaster oven beside the bed. An extension cord powers his bed light, the ancient radio and his black and white TV. A shotgun provides protection. Hunters who have leased hunting rights on the family land cut his firewood each fall.
Jonnie Richardson hasn't seen a doctor in 20 years. The only one he trusted moved away. No dentist will come to the old house. "My teeth hurt me right smart," he said. "Couple of times they put me in a truck and took me to a dentist to have some pulled. It just wore me out."

This clipping has been in my Sweet Assorted tin box since it first appeared in the *Seattle Times* thirty years ago. I've removed it from the box perhaps four times in all those years and have wondered about it, and about Jonnie Richardson. What was his real reason for going to bed and not getting up? Surely it was more than that he was "feeling poorly." He was only sixteen when he took to bed; had he been middle-aged, you could think that he'd given up on life and it just wasn't worth the effort. Sometimes I'd look at the clipping and think he was a self-indulgent jerk for lying there and forcing others to take care of him. At other times, I'd feel sorry for him, imagine some big secret, an unbearable hurt that had sent him to bed forever. At yet other times, I could see him at the centre of some absurdist existential novel.
So lately, when I decided to catalogue the contents of the Sweet Assorted box, I thought I'd look into the mystery of Jonnie Richardson. I made some phone calls to Laurel Springs, North Carolina, and surrounding towns like Sparta and West Jefferson.

The first four people I spoke with had no memory or knowledge of Jonnie Richardson. Finally, I located the executive director of the Alleghany County Chamber of Commerce and Visitor's Center, one Bob Bamberg, who'd been a journalist and had written about Jonnie in the '90s.

"I was the editor of a local weekly paper, and once a day, I'd go across the street, kitty-corner to my office to the drugstore to get my candy bar. One time I saw this lady—we called her 'Red'—reading some paper like the *National Enquirer* or *News of the World*, something like that. I said to her, 'How come you reading that and not my paper?' She said, 'Well, if you ever run a story like what's in here, I will.'

"Well, one day a year or so later I go over for my candy bar, and Red is in there, and when she sees me, she holds up her newspaper and shakes it and says, 'Here, look at this.'

"It was all about this local man being in bed for fifty years, so I went and found him and wrote him up."

Bamberg told me he would search for those stories and if he found them, would mail them to me.

He was true to his word.

Bamberg's story appeared in the *Golden Post*, a tabloid supplement to the *Jefferson Post* that featured stories on older people. The story appeared in the May 31, 1994, issue, and Mr. Richardson's first name is spelled with an "h."

Johnnie's cabin was in a remote part of eastern Ashe County, south of Scottville. There were six rooms, but—of course—he confined himself to the bed in one of them. Richardson let the reporter in using a stick to unlatch the cabin door. Bamberg found him at "78…frail looking but energetic." Although "his long-atrophied legs make little impression on the covers," Bamberg found Johnnie's upper body displayed a "limberness more characteristic of a practitioner of yoga."

Alongside his bed, Richardson had everything he needed at arms' length. He had various strings and wires, tubes and buckets arranged to take care of his needs. When Bamberg allowed as how being bedbound must be a hardship, Richardson replied, "Ah, you get used to it."

When Johnnie's sister, Bessie, mentioned in the previous article, got so frail she had to go into a nursing home, her work was taken over by a nephew and hunters who would call by now and again. At the time of Bamberg's article, an aide from the Ashe Services for Aging In-Home visited twice a week.

There is some interesting information in Bamberg's article about Richardson's early days and those of his ancestors. His paternal grandparents came into the area in 1869, and settled on 145 acres purchased for $275. His parents ran a self-sufficient operation, planting gardens and raising cattle and sheep. "My mother sheared the sheep," Johnnie recalled. "Corded the wool, made it into rolls; spun it and twisted the thread and knit our stockings on knitting needles."

Nearly everything used on the farm was made on the farm, including homemade lye soap and boneset tea. Toothaches were treated with wet but hot ashes.

Hard to imagine from the more recent photographs of Richardson that he would ever have been, as he described himself, "a stout boy." But there in Bamberg's article is a photograph of him in bed at age sixteen; he has a round face and dark hair. His mother is standing at his side, an arm resting on the bedstead. Mrs. Richardson, Carrie, had only one eye, her right. Johnnie's father, Brady, was also missing an eye, his left, having lost it while breaking up rock on a road-construction gang.

In the two months prior to Bamberg's article being published, Johnnie had spilled scalding hot water on himself on two occasions. As well, he was losing strength in his hands and his eyes watered when he tried to read. There was talk of moving him to a nursing home, but he wasn't having any of it. "I'm not going anywhere unless I have to and I can't think of a time when I'd have to."

In a letter to me, Bamberg writes, "As best as I remember, Johnnie died two or three years after the article was published."

TAKE 11

3" X 5" SHEET OF LINED PAPER TORN FROM NOTEBOOK; MY HANDWRITING

One side reads, "Sentenced to 2 yrs. For counselling young men to avoid conscription (which she never did) to be followed by deportation (so was Berkman). Her to Missouri State Prison; Him to Atlanta.

"Upon release deported under Palmer Raid (Attny General Mitchell Palmer) deportation of aliens; anti-subversive—tho E.G. sent away illegally as she was U.S. citizen by marriage Dec 21, 1919."

This is obviously about Emma Goldman, my heroine.

Emma Goldman fought injustice wherever and whenever it raised its head, which was just about everywhere and all the time. She suffered for her positions, which (as she confesses in her autobiography, *Living My Life*) were occasionally misguided. But she was never a small "l," much less large "L," liberal, and bourgeois feminism was anathema to her. She did not, for instance, support the suffragette movement. What good was the right to vote when the system was thoroughly corrupt and there was no one to vote for? She was an early supporter of the Russian Revolution, and then she was deported to the country of her birth. The result was her great book, *My Disillusionment in Russia*.

We need her likes now in this era of jejune protest and left-wing media clowns.

On the back of this piece of paper, I've scrawled, "Jimmy Rowles singing 'Old Fashioned.'"

TAKE 12

PHOTOGRAPH OF MAN ON THE MOON

I set my $35 35-millimetre junkshop camera on a kitchen chair by the television in the front room of a house on Delaware Avenue in Toronto. I turned the lights out and shot several pictures of the moon landing. This one shows Neil Armstrong at the left centre of the screen. The caption at the bottom: LIVE FROM MOON. At the top left is Richard Nixon in profile with the telephone in his left hand.

TAKE 13

VIETNAMESE LOTTERY TICKET

It cost 2000 dong. I might have won the car, but I didn't.

I did, however, have a little luck later that week when I landed a bit in a television commercial for a foot-massage machine. I gave my minuscule fee to a friend of mine, a Cambodian refugee in Saigon, so that he could get his motorbike fixed and make some money taking tourists around town.

TAKE 14

8½" X 11" LINED NOTEBOOK PAGE

I vaguely remember scribbling some of this in one place or another on East Hastings Street; must have been 1986.

- The girl running for the bus tonight, two car loads of guys honking, calling to her...
- Moving into this neighbourhood, Alexander St. A hundred years ago, these houses all brothels, madams' names in tiles on vestibule floor—co-op housing project named for a Madame, Maria Gomez
- The hookers: girl in Chinese café with her boyfriend—pimp—every time she leaves, calls to him— "I wuff oooh"—he replies belligerently, embarrassed, "Yeah, me too," or curtly, "I love you too." He has stubble of hair on head, dressed in black—her in tight pants, imitation fur jacket, sweater underneath that doesn't cover navel, heels, she struts back and forth out front, pouty, with the chubbiness of a precocious little girl, pushing her tummy out, rolling her hips—

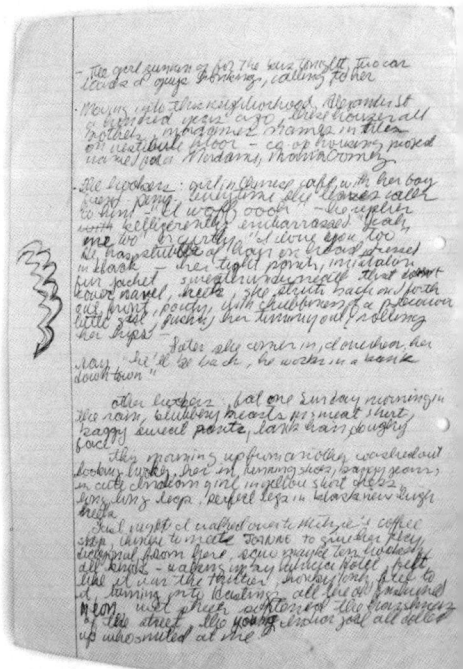

- Later she comes in; I hear her say, "He'll be back, he works in a bank downtown."

Other hookers: fat one Sunday morning in the rain, blubbery breasts in sweat shirt, baggy sweat pants, lank hair, doughy face.

This morning up front, another washed-out looking hooker (*note: I don't understand* that line either; perhaps the "*up*" should be an "*out*") her in running shoes, baggy jeans. Cute Indian girl in yellow short dress, long long legs, perfect legs in black new high heels.

Last night I walked over to Mitzie's coffee shop, Chinese, to meet Joanne give her _____ (indecipherable), diagonal from here, saw maybe ten hookers all kinds—walking up by Patricia Hotel, felt like it was the '30s, honky-tonk feel to it, turning onto Hastings all the old-fashioned neon, wet streets softened the harshness, the young Indian girl all dolled up who smiled at me.

TAKE 15

A SORT OF COLLAGE ON THICK WHITE PAPER, SUCH AS WOULD BE IN A SKETCH PAD

The collage contains the receipt for admission to the Museo Casa Diego Rivera in Guanajuato, Gto. (No. 87944). It's pasted on horizontally. Below it, placed vertically, is a small photograph of one of my early art pieces. I remember it was called *Mr. I Been Everywhere*. The character has a pot lid for a head and a quarter section of a globe of the world for a stomach. He has on shades, and from where his "ears" would be, dangle two baggage tags. On the "ground" at the base of the sculpture is his suitcase.

Next to this is most of a general-admission ticket to the Montreal Expos' City Island Park in Daytona Beach, Florida. This probably dates from the period 1977 to 1981, when I was wintering in St. Augustine, forty miles north of Daytona Beach. I once got asked by a magazine to interview the Expos' star catcher Gary Carter, which I did at his apartment. Another time, a more interesting time, was spent talking with the great Rod Carew, who would win the batting championship seven times and be voted into the Baseball Hall of Fame, a very intelligent guy who told me about all the troubles he had living in his upscale suburb near Minneapolis with his white wife.

Below these, also placed vertically, are two scraps from a news clipping. One reads like a Burroughs cut-up, which it is, I suppose. The other makes sense, to wit: "He now lives back inside the park, renovating the dilapidated old ranger's house where he grew up. Soon after moving in, he had to scare away two enormous lionesses who tried to attack him as he slept on the verandah."

Between this fragment and the cut-up is a bit of pink paint (or maybe it's a smeared lipstick kiss) and below that is a swath of green paint and my signature in black ink. The cut-up:

> Says Indian advocacy
> Sembles that of environ
> Groups. That's because
> Clout, even with money. I
> Must convince policymaker
> Cause has broad support
> Tory in last November's cast

TAKE 16

KILLIELERSUNERMI ALLAGARTAQ; OR, IN DANISH, RATIONERINGSARK (FOR AUGUST 1981)

This is what remains of my liquor-rationing card for the month during which my visit to Greenland occurred. I had learned that there were going to be flights from Canada to Greenland, and I wanted to be on one of them. As per my habit, I went somewhere that I was curious about and hoped to write about.

For a brief time, a flight connected the town formerly known as Frobisher Bay to Nuuk, or Godthåb in Danish. I flew from the CARP base in Ottawa to Frobisher Bay, which then consisted of a scattering of shacks surrounding the Federal Government Building. I was put in mind of a litter of puppies surrounding the mother, the big bitch. In my ignorance, I figured if this northern-Canada town looked so woebegone, then Greenland would surely be a sad, bedraggled sight. In reality, Nuuk was a neat, well-maintained town that wouldn't be out of place on the outskirts of Copenhagen. There were medium-rise apartment buildings, and my first afternoon there, I saw two Inuit men dragging part of a walrus carcass along the road between apartment buildings.

But arriving at the tiny airport, I was disappointed that the customs official had gone home. The daily flight from Denmark had come and gone, so the official, it was explained to me, figured it wasn't worthwhile to wait around to stamp in one or two visitors from Canada. I got a ride into town with one of the airline ticket sellers, and she stopped at the official's home. I wanted that Greenland stamp in my passport. But he wasn't home, either.

The little town was surrounded on three sides by dark-blue water dotted by icebergs of the whitest white I had ever seen or imagined. There was a graveyard next to the old church, and the crosses rolled downhill to the water. There was green grass, too, and I saw even more of it when I went out on a boat exploring local fjords.

I had a good time and met plenty of people. I even appeared in an Inuit rock video—I was only vaguely aware at the time that there were such things as music videos. I had met the musicians in a pub. The next day, we went out to an iceberg, in a boat filled with instruments, speakers and electronic gear, as well as a desk, chair, typewriter and metal wastepaper basket. I was to play the part of the uptight bureaucrat sent over from Copenhagen. The musicians danced around me, lip-synching their song, which was a satire on Danish rule. It was funny seeing the speakers set up on the ice, cords stuck into ice mounds. In frustration, I ripped page after page from the typewriter and tossed them toward the wastepaper basket.

I had gotten talking to these guys while watching a spontaneous striptease in the pub on my first night in town. A couple of Inuit women were sitting close by. A few minutes after I arrived, one jumped up and started dancing to the recorded music. After a moment, she grabbed at the bottom of her sweater and pulled it up, exposing her navel, the rest of her stomach and then her bra. Her friend called the waitress over as she poured her bottle of beer and the dancer's bottle of beer over the dancer's head. The waitress appeared at the same time that both bottles were drained. The dancer stopped, and her friend handed the waitress her monthly ration card, which was divided into squares, each one with "1

POINT" on it. One point=one drink. The waitress took the card, and with the scissors fastened to a string around her neck, proceeded to cut out one coupon. After that was done, she handed over one bottle of beer. The friend took it and raised it, started pouring slowly, and only then did the dancer get in motion. She got the sweater off, threw it on the floor and began working on her jeans. Bottle empty, the dancing stopped, another coupon was cut out, the beer proffered and poured, and the dancing resumed. This went on until the dancer was down to her skimpy panties and the waitress called a halt to the proceedings. It really was a tease. The dancer wrapped her sweater around her hips and walked bare breasted to the women's room.

Hearing me talk to the waitress, the musicians figured I wasn't Danish and, therefore, might be worth speaking to. They seemed surprised to learn that there is not much stripping by bar patrons in Canada.

TAKE 17

PIECE OF OFF-WHITE PLAIN PAPER, 4" X 9", FOLDED IN HALF, LENGTHWISE; A QUOTE ON EACH HALF, ONE IN BLUE, ONE IN BLACK INK, WRITTEN BY ME

The one in blue ink reads, "Art does not lie down in the bed that is made for it. It runs away as soon as one says its name; it lives to be incognito. Its best moments are when it forgets what it is called." I don't attribute this, but it is from the artist Jean Dubuffet. Art does not pay attention.

In black ink: "Serve the dinner backward, do anything—but for goodness sake, do something weird." Elsa Maxwell.

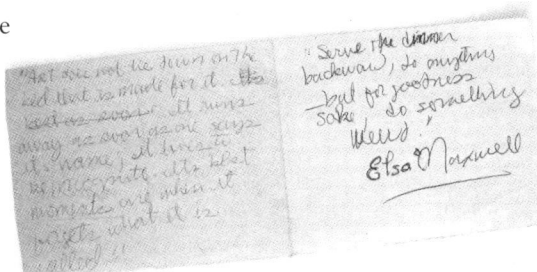

TAKE 18

SKETCHES FOR AN ART PIECE, AN ASSEMBLAGE THAT I HOPED TO MAKE BUT NEVER HAVE

There is a crucifix inside a frame; there were to be wristwatches, clock parts, skulls, tiny plastic babies and caskets. Below this sketch is one of a figure who was, perhaps, to be on the crucifix. At first I drew him with both legs straight down, as if standing; then I scratched out the left leg and re-did it so the leg is raised. He—I guess it's a he—is waving his left hand.

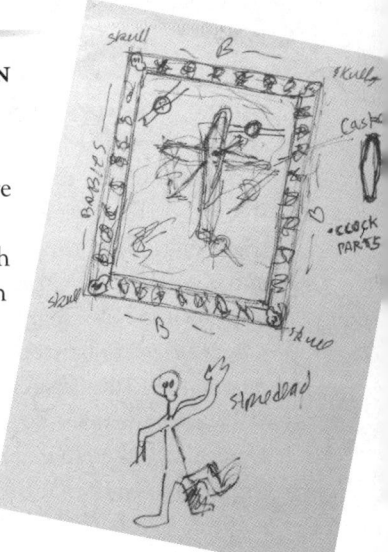

TAKE 19

A SMALL BOOK, THE SPINE AND CORNERS BOUND IN BLUE LEATHER WITH CHINESE DESIGNS PRINTED ON BLUE CLOTH IN BETWEEN. DIARY IS WRITTEN ON THE SPINE. AT THE BACK OF THE DIARY I HAVE PRINTED, "FOUND AT A DUMP UP THE BC COAST, 1 NOV '02."

I remember coming upon this one cloudy day, but it seems to me I actually found it while walking on the two-lane highway before the turnoff to the dump. It's a girl's diary, neatly written for the first few pages, then not-so-neatly written, and finally becomes just scratches and scrawls.

I got into the habit of picking up letters from the streets in the early '70s. The first time was in the west end of Vancouver. I found an invitation to a dinner hosted by the Lieutenant-Governor of British Columbia. Had the recipient lost the invitation? Or just tossed it away? The litterbug. As I bent to retrieve that piece of paper, I thought of the "Count," with whom I had tramped the roads of upper New York State when I was just a kid. He gave these items careful attention, whether they were letters, advertisements for a tune-up, or half of a paperback war novel. He'd read them and throw them away (in the proper receptacles). After picking up that invitation, I decided to start my own collection, but of letters only, and I have done so, naming this material, kept in folders, "Pages from the Sidewalks of Life," in memory of that gentle, nutty, displaced White Russian. He had used the phrase when I inquired as to why he was interested in that kind of thing. "Ah, Jimmy," he said, "but this is the real literature, these pages from the sidewalks of life."

For at least two decades, I plucked paper from the street. I was particularly interested in letters, but anything handwritten appealed to me, and I'd be plucking still if people still wrote letters or anything at all by hand. It has been nearly a decade since I've found anything other than a shopping list or half a page of a homework assignment in North America. In fact, the diary is probably the last thing I came across on these shores. I was able to extend my predilection a few years during trips to Asia and, in December 2011, I found a very interesting page in Moscow, but have absolutely no idea what it's all about, although I suspect it has something to do with Kim Kardashian, whoever that is. (Dear editor: I'm only kidding. Not about not knowing who K.K. is, but about her being the focus of the letter. It's actually about Victor Serge's love life.)

But now, alas, there is nothing. I could search through trash containers at the post office and not find anything. (That would also be cheating.) It is sad to admit this and what it means not only for me but the world in general: just another example of the disappearance of texture in the world.

The diary, not being a letter, and being too thick for a folder, I tossed in my Peak Frean box.

TAKE 20

RECEIPT FOR TWO NIGHTS AT THE TRINIDAD HILTON HOTEL, BEGINNING 25 MAY 1988

I was in Trinidad to cover the world's light-heavyweight championship bout between former champion Leslie Stewart of Trinidad and the current crown holder, Don Lalonde of Canada. The two pieces I wrote appeared first in a newspaper; I later expanded the material and included it in a book on boxing called *Flesh and Blood*.

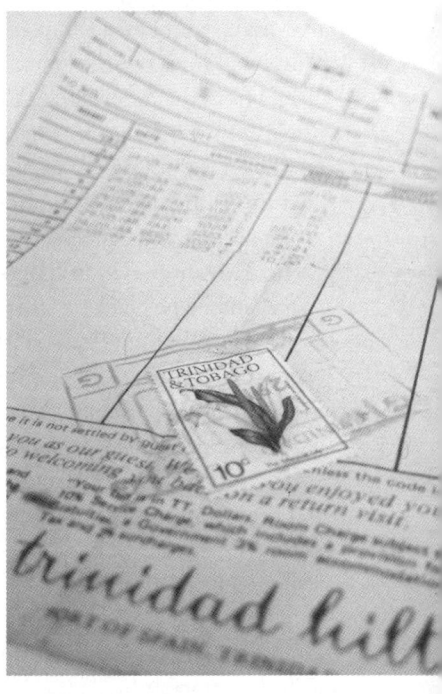

I had a great time in Trinidad, meeting and hanging around with famous and notorious figures from the boxing world. These ranged from Lalonde himself to legendary characters such as ninety-four-year-old manager and matchmaker Marty Cohen, manager Dave Wolf, Don Majeski, a behind-the-scenes figure known as The Vampire, referee Marty Denkin (who was the referee in the movie *Rocky IV*, whom I had met on the set) and numerous others. Then there were various shadier characters, which is another story. (As the editor seems quite curious about these shady characters, I'll mention one. This guy supplied hookers to high rollers; the hookers reported back to him with information about the men's sexual habits and where they hid their wallets. This latter bit was of use when he dispatched hotel thieves to their rooms.) There was one guy; I had no idea who he was, though he was a friendly sort and had plenty of what it takes to make the world go around. He had been supplied with one of these high-priced hookers, a tall, coffee-coloured woman of mixed Indian and African ancestry. When he found out that the television cameras would be across the ring from where he sat and would be pointed his way, he was very upset. "My wife will be watching in hopes of seeing me at ringside. But she'll go nuts if she sees me with the girl. Do me a favour. You take her; let her sit with you. Keep her." I declined his most generous offer.

The Trinidad Hilton was known as the Upside Down Hotel because the lobby was on the top floor. There was a fitness centre advertised. I decided to use it prior to plunging into this milieu, which I knew would require lots of drinking and late nights. The concierge directed me to a small cottage outside the main hotel. Inside the cottage were two rusty barbells and two folding chairs on which sat two very large Trinidadian women. There wasn't room for all of us, so one woman moved her chair to the doorway. Both women proceeded to watch my activities intently. They followed the barbell from the floor to its raised position over my head. They assessed me conscientiously. One lady said I would no doubt feel better if I took my shirt off. I excused myself and told them I had forgotten I needed to make a phone call, and left. My hands were covered with rust.

On the hotel receipt, there is a very nice 10¢ Trinidad and Tobago stamp of a Maraval Lily.

TAKE 21

STRIP OF TORN WHITE PAPER

On one side, I've jotted a line from Rimbaud, although I don't attribute the little guttersnipe: "One night, I sat Beauty on my knee—and I found her bitter. And I insulted her."

Underneath this, I've scrawled, "In St. Augustine we took two black Beauties on our knees…"

The strip of paper is torn through the top part of a drawing in red pen; there appear eyebrows, the top of a pointy head and a tuft of hair.

On the other side of the strip, in black ink, I've written the opening line from a song called "Without Love," probably heard on the radio, and sung by Rosemary Clooney: "…is a pleasure unemployed."

TAKE 22

NEW YORK TIMES OBIT, AUGUST 9, 1996: "HERBERT HUNCKE, THE HIPSTER WHO DEFINED 'BEAT' DIES AT 81"

Jack Kerouac and Neal Cassady were thirty years gone, and the remaining members of the beat generation were beginning to pass on in bunches. Huncke would soon be followed by Burroughs, Ginsberg and Corso.

The obit refers to Huncke as "the charismatic street hustler, petty thief and perennial drug addict who enthralled and inspired a galaxy of acclaimed writers and gave the Beat Generation its name...who died of congestive heart failure at Beth Israel Hospital..." The *Times* writer points out the man's last name "rhymes with junkie" and that he "gave William S. Burroughs his first fix...introduced Jack Kerouac to the term 'beat' and...guided Allen Ginsberg and John Clellon Holmes through the netherworld of Times Square in the 1940s. They in turn made him 'an icon of his times,' using him in their books."

Born into a middle-class family (his father owned a machine-parts distributing company) Huncke, who ran away from home in his teens, "said he was using drugs as early as twelve, selling sex by the time he was sixteen, stealing virtually anything his (sic) throughout his life and never once apologizing for a moment of it."

Huncke was the protagonist of Burroughs's debut novel, *Junkie*. The first time Huncke saw the future great writer was when Burroughs appeared at the door of the apartment wanting to sell a sawed-off shotgun. Huncke took one look at him and said to his roommate, "Get rid of him, he's the FBI."

I met him only once, in 1967 or '68. I was living with two friends in a seven-room apartment in the old Lower East Side. One day, returning home, I met a man with jet-black, combed-back hair, wearing a black leather jacket, coming down the stairs. He smiled and very politely asked if I could lend him some money. When I told him that I could not, he smiled again and continued on his way.

When I reached the apartment, my friend asked if I'd seen the old greaser-looking guy. When I nodded, he said, "That was the immortal Herbert Huncke. Jack Kerouac must have been a saint to find anything good to say about that guy."

Maybe so, but Huncke, although he might steal from his friends for a fix, never ratted anybody out, even when it would have spared him months of jail time.

Interestingly, below the essay on Huncke is an ad for a funeral director, with the slogan, "Leaders in Funeral Pre-Planning for Generations…"

TAKE 23

NEWSPAPER PHOTO: BORIS YELTSIN, A SECRETARY, MEN IN SUITS AND TIES IN THE BACKGROUND

Cut line is headed "DON'T DO THAT" and comments that the secretary is jumping with surprise as the Russian president "pinches her between the shoulder blades" before a news conference.

Her expression is a priceless one of shock. What Yeltsin is really doing, one supposes, is snapping her bra strap. He has an evil, sneaky look on his face.

DON'T DO THAT — A secretary jumps with surprise when Russian President Boris Yeltsin pinches her between the shoulder blades as he prepares for a news conference in Moscow yesterday. *(Reuters)*

TAKE 24

PHOTOCOPY OF AD RECEIPT WITH QUOTATION ON REVERSE SIDE

This is the bottom half of a receipt from a newspaper—a Vancouver paper, probably the *Sun*—for a notice advertising for sale a 1967 Plymouth Fury. This would have been placed in late 1982. It has my name and address on Oxford Street, Vancouver. Asking price is $400.

I had moved to Vancouver the previous December, but as there was a zero vacancy rate, I had to divide my time bunking with friends in town and visiting others in Seattle. I bought the car and a seventeen-foot trailer in Washington. Come Spring, I set the trailer up on a pad in a field near Duncan, B.C., and sat outside in rare good weather to work on my biography of Charles Bedaux.

On the other side of this scrap of paper is a quote from Dick Wellstood, who I've described as a "stride piano player." I seem to recall he wrote some autobiographical pieces for a music magazine. "You play the piano and people applaud, they throw money, they throw babies up onstage and tell you how great you are. But writing, you do it and stick it in an envelope and that's it. There's no applause."

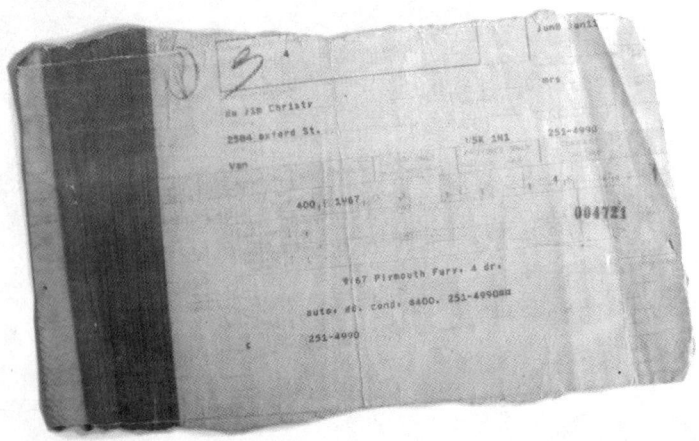

TAKE 25

THREE ROLLING STONES 45 RPM RECORDS ON THE DECCA INDIGO LABEL BUT IN THREE DIFFERENT PAPER SLEEVES: DECCA, MERCURY, LONDON

The disks are "Let's Spend the Night Together"/"Ruby Tuesday"; "Get Off of My Cloud"/"The Singer Not the Song"; "The Last Time"/"Play with Fire." The first two songs are copyrighted 1967; the others, 1965.

I picked these up at the Terminal Avenue Flea Market in Vancouver. Although I like (and liked) the Rolling Stones, I've never been a fan. Maybe I thought these sides would be worth some money.

A recent Internet check informs me that they'd go for a whopping $30 each.

TAKE 26

PHOTO TAKEN AT BUKOWSKI'S BAR & BISTRO ON COMMERCIAL DRIVE IN VANCOUVER, AFTER I DID MY POETRY WITH A JAZZ BAND

I'm sitting next to a Russian sculptor, whose name I can't recall. Standing behind us are Ian Hannington, who at the time was an editor with the *Georgia Straight*, and my good buddy Paul Murphy, who used to be an organizer for the New Democratic Party, and before that, a veteran of hundreds of parachute jumps in the Korean War. Murphy and I travelled together, drank together, traded books and had great times. He was that rare thing, a real stand-up guy. Murphy is holding a drink—a pint of Guinness, I believe. Murphy, who died in 2005, was always holding a drink. I miss him dearly. I don't know who took the picture.

TAKE 27

PAGE TORN FROM A LARGE "DAY BOOK"

I found this outside a motel near some town in Oregon. I was driving around looking for unusual homes and gardens for a book that came to be called *Strange Sites*.

The lone page has Tuesday, May 27, on one side; the 28th on the other. The 28th is blank, but there are two lines written under the 27th: "Went to Zapps tonight to ladies' night with Leona. Met Ed Lowe."

Well, I wonder what happened. Did they begin a long romance? Maybe they're married still. Or perhaps they had a one-night stand, and that stand took place in that very motel.

What was Ed Lowe doing at Zapps on ladies' night? Maybe guys were there waiting outside at closing time.

TAKE 28

5" X 7" BLACK-AND-WHITE PHOTOGRAPH, PROBABLY TAKEN IN THE LATE 1940S THAT SHOWS A JEEP-LIKE SEDAN APPROACHING A STEEP HILL ON A ROUGH DIRT ROAD CRUDELY SLASHED THROUGH THE FOREST

Affixed to the back of the picture is a strip, upon which is typed "'Suicide Hill—Prepare to meet thy maker' was the sign at the bottom of one steep grade on the original army supply road. The Alaska Highway was built in just over eight months and grades like these were not uncommon. Vast improvements were undertaken by the U.S. Roads administration, Canadian Army and Canadian Contractors before the road was opened to the public in 1949."

Credit line: Fort St. John, North Peace Museum Archives.

I wrote a book about the Alaska Highway and the land through which it passes: *Rough Road to the North* (Doubleday, 1980). This must be a photograph that I collected during my research. I should note that in 1993, I was sent by *Equinox* magazine to do a piece on the fiftieth anniversary of the completion of the road that runs from Dawson Creek, B.C., to Fairbanks, Alaska. During the trip, I met an old native man who had been around during the construction days and who solemnly told me about the soldiers he had encountered, "Yes, the first white person I ever met was a black man."

TAKE 29

POEM WRITTEN ON AIRPLANE, FLIGHT FROM VANCOUVER TO WHITEHORSE, IN THE EARLY '70S

I lived in the Yukon off and on for years. Poem was written with ballpoint pen on a page torn from a spiral notebook, perforations at the top:

Cartoon Character
Fool in a silver bird
Over Lake Laberge
30,000 feet and descending
To the left the river—emerald
Feathered by banks of snow

And now the roofs of Whitehorse

So I really have done it
Left you 4,000 miles away
To the right over Grey Mtn.
Wispy clouds taunt,
Ask me Why.

TAKE 30

MAPLE LEAF GARDENS, WORKING PASS

I was there, on May 10, 1971, to cover the George Chuvalo—Jimmy Ellis heavyweight fight, the winner to get a shot at Muhammed Ali's title. Ellis won.

I had met George Chuvalo earlier, during his training sessions, and consider myself fortunate to have run into him more than a couple of times over the years. I regard him as a hero, not only for his boxing career but also because of all he has gone through and survived, handling his numerous personal tragedies with great dignity.

But he is, in my opinion, absolutely wrong about the Klitschko brothers, heavyweight champs, Wladimir and Vitali. The last time I saw Chuvalo was at the Boxing Gym on Dundas West in Toronto, in 2011. He declared that neither Vitali or Wladimir could have stood up to the heavyweights of his era. I humbly begged to differ. No one at his peak, including Muhammed Ali, could have beaten Vitali Klitschko.

TAKE 31

PHOTOCOPY OF ARTICLE FROM THE LONDON FREE PRESS, MARCH 1939: "LONDONER TURNED DOWN OFFER OF PLACE IN CREW OF HALLIBURTON'S JUNK"

A picture caption reads, "Top picture is the last photograph taken of the *Sea Dragon*, Richard Halliburton's $20,000 Chinese junk, destined for the World's Fair at San Francisco, but now unreported for several days following a typhoon east of Midway Island in the Pacific Ocean. She sailed from Hong Kong March 4 when this picture was taken. It was sent to The London Free Press by W. J. Rowland, of London, now on a tour of the Orient. The Chinese characters at the stern read 'Sea Dragon, Hong Kong,' her port of registry. The little ship of fifty tons was, as Halliburton said, 'a mixture of Chinese junk, Spanish galleon and Halliburton.' Was there something ominous in the comment of the Hong Kong sailorman who, after inspecting her in the water, remarked: 'Something of her sailing qualities may have been sacrificed'? Below—Just before the *Sea Dragon* sailed, Richard Halliburton posed for this picture with Mr. Rowland. Mr. Halliburton is at the left; Mr. Rowland at the right. In the centre is John B. Flagg, first mate."

Not many people know of Richard Halliburton these days and even those who do cannot imagine just how famous he was in the '20s and '30s. He was a dashing swashbuckler, every boy's hero, and it was the dream of every boy to be just like him. He went on the most incredible adventures, climbed mountains, sailed the seas, hiked into forbidden territory. He swam in c-notes, swam the Hellespont, and is the only person ever to swim the entire Panama Canal. Also, he was blond and handsome and totally without fear.

When he sailed out of Hong Kong, he was thirty-nine years old, and he was never heard from again.

As for John Rowland, who didn't go with him on the *Sea Dragon*, I met him in 1992 in Kelowna, B.C. I was writing a weekly column for the paper, the *Courier*, and he left a note at the office: "Are you

HONG KONG   MARCH 1939

Sails on Fateful Voyage

Top picture is the last photograph taken of the Sea Dragon, Richard Halliburton's $20,000 Chinese junk, destined for the World's Fair at San Francisco, but now unreported for several days following a typhoon east of Midway Island, in the Pacific Ocean. She sailed from Hong Kong March 4, when this picture was taken. It was sent to The London Free Press by W. J. Rowland, of London, now on a tour of the Orient. The Chinese characters at the stern read "Sea Dragon, Hong Kong," her port of registry. The little ship of 50 tons was, as Halliburton said, "a mixture of Chinese junk, Spanish galleon, and Halliburton." Was there something ominous in the comment of Hong Kong sailormen who, after inspecting her in the water, remarked: "Something of her sailing qualities may have been sacrificed"? Below—Just before the Sea Dragon sailed, Richard Halliburton posed for this picture with Mr. Rowland. Mr. Halliburton is at the left; Mr. Rowland at the right; in the centre is John B. Flagg, first mate.

Londoner Turned Down Offer of Place In Crew Of Halliburton's Junk

the same Jim Christy who was in the Yukon? I once wrote a letter coming to your defence. Give me a call, if you please."

Twelve years previously, the *Globe and Mail* ran a series of excerpts from my book about the Alaska Highway and the country through which it passes. One of the pieces concerns a little incident at Carcross, Y.T. I was riding in the caboose on the narrow-gauge Yukon White Pass Route train from Skagway, and its progress was halted by drifting snow. So I borrowed a pair of snowshoes and hiked a couple of kilometres to the hotel at Carcross. The hotel had been built by Tagish Charlie, one of the three men whose gold discovery started the Klondike Gold Rush. A ship's captain left his parrot with Tagish Charlie when he went on his honeymoon Outside. The parrot had been a wedding gift for his bride. The couple were going to sail down to San Francisco and be back in two months. That was in 1901 or '02. They never returned. The ship went down off the coast of Oregon. There were no survivors.

The bird was still there in its cage at the hotel, an angry, scrofulous creature. It tolerated women and children, by which I mean it would not try to attack them. But should a man get near the cage, the ugly thing screamed, threw itself against the bars and tried to get at him.

The day after the piece describing this episode appeared, a man wrote a letter to the paper that keeping just this side of libel, called me a liar, said I made the whole thing up and why wasn't the august *Globe and Mail* acting more responsibly.

It seems as if there is always someone around to insinuate that one is a liar; but at least this guy came out with it. Anyway, the next day, the *Globe* ran a letter in my defence: the writer of the letter had spent a lot of time in those parts, been in that hotel, and not only was he familiar with the parrot, he was also reminded of it every day, every hour, because the damn thing had bitten off half of his pinkie finger. The letter was signed "John Rowland."

So twelve years later, when I got that note from John Rowland, I telephoned him, and he invited me to come see him. He was a husky, rugged man, about six-feet-two, with a florid, sunbaked face and snow-white hair. I later realized that he was eighty years old but would have passed for a healthy fellow twenty years younger. His home overlooked Lake Okanagan, and we sat on his terrace, drank gin and tonics and kept an eye out for Ogopogo. Naturally, we talked about the Yukon and the characters we'd met in different decades. John had gone up there in 1934 on the most peculiar of errands: to sell subscriptions to the brand new *Newsweek* magazine.

His job consisted of more than calling door to door in Whitehorse and Dawson City. In fact, had he sold a subscription to every household, he wouldn't have made much money. So he also travelled the waterways by canoe, stopping at any cabin he could spot or any back in the bush that he heard about, the idea being to spread the news about the magazine. Along the way, he met numerous women home all alone while their husbands were panning on the creeks or tending the trap lines. It was during these years that he had his encounter with the parrot at Carcross.

While reciting his adventures, he brought up the episode with Halliburton. "I ran into him in Hong Kong. When he found out I had some experience on boats, he offered me the job. The whole notion of the adventure really thrilled me. I mean, the man was adventure personified. Even though he was a little peculiar…"

Rowland paused. I said, "You mean because he was gay?"

He looked at me with surprise. "Well, he never approached me, but there were things in his mannerisms. I didn't know for sure. But I figured it wouldn't be a problem. I looked forward to the trip, but that was before I ever saw the ship. Even after I did, I still wanted to go—I mean he was famous and he'd write about the adventure—but the night before we were to leave, I had a premonition. You can see by that newspaper story I gave you that the photo was taken on the 4th of March, and he sailed on the 5th. So I went and woke him up at dawn and told him I was backing out. He was angry, to say the least. I warned him to make drastic changes to the ship, but he said he couldn't delay any longer."

Every now and again, Rowland would telephone me in Kelowna and say, "It's about time we looked for Ogopogo again." Which was my invitation to drink gin and tonics at his place. He was quite a guy and a great storyteller.

I left town but I saw John Rowland again, thirteen years later.

I was invited to read poetry in West Vancouver at a place called the Honeymoon Cottage. On the telephone, the organizer asked me if I knew anything about the place. When I told her that I did not, she explained that the last remaining member of a formerly prominent family had donated the waterfront house to the town, which turned it into an arts centre.

On the evening of the reading, I appeared at the cottage twenty minutes late, a victim once more of the B.C. ferry system. The organizer approached as I entered the building and gently reproached me: "You said you didn't know anything about the Honeymoon Cottage, but then I find out you even know the man who donated it."

"What?"

"A man named John Rowland."

At first, the name was unfamiliar.

"He said you know each other from the Yukon and the Okanagan."

I remembered and looked around the room.

"That's him over there."

She pointed to a big, gaunt old man, wearing a suit that was much too large for him. He was a rawboned coot with an irascible look in his eyes. When he saw me, he banged the point of his cane on the floor and called, "You're late, Christy!"

Even though he looked nothing like the man I had met thirteen years earlier, I knew it was John Rowland. I kept looking at him, trying to see the burly man I had known.

After I did some preliminary adlibbing and read a few poems, Rowland's loud but creaky voice called out, "Read some Yukon stuff!"

I did that. "That's the ticket!" he called after the first one.

Then after the second poem, he said, "Oh, her. I think I knew her, Josie Mother of Bear."

There are always ladies in their sixties who attend these readings, no matter the poet nor the material. The ladies at this reading kept turning to look at Rowland and scowl their displeasure. One even shushed him. He paid no attention.

"Say, Jim. Did you go out with the Lady that's Known as Lou?"

"No, John. That must have been you. She was before my time."

He actually slapped his boney-looking thigh and laughed. "That's right. That's right!"

When I was halfway through the next one, he shouted out a question. "What was it about the piano player's hands?"

He was making a reference to Robert Service.

"They were gnarled," I answered. "And drove the women wild."

Well, John's rambunctiousness infected the others to some mild degree, and it turned into a spirited event.

When I was done, he came up and got my shoulders in a grip with his big hands and squeezed with his own long, gnarled fingers. We started talking about the Yukon and Halliburton while the others just watched. It was a special moment, and I realized as we went back and forth that John Rowland had to be in his nineties and thus was the last representative of another era.

We walked outside together, him bent forward just a little bit and aerating the soil with the point of his cane. "You know that woman you're with, she's quite a looker. Makes me wish I was thirty years younger, well, forty maybe."

We said our goodbyes and shook hands, and John went off toward the sea walk. He reminded me of some eternal old salt headed for a tavern on the waterfront to spin yarns with others just like him.

He died three months later, age ninety-four.

COLOUR PICTURE POSTCARD OF A DECORATED VAN; ABOVE THE VAN IS A CAPTION: "COPY CAT"

The vehicle belongs to the artist, and my friend, Ken Gerberick. On the other side of the postcard is printed:
"1979 Ford Econoline created to represent over 30 different ART VECHICLES including the artist's 1st three ART CARS. 90% of the items on this ART VAN came out of the garbage around Ken's home in Vancouver, B.C. It took one of four 2nd place honours at the 1998 ART CAR WEEKEND in HOUSTON, TX."

I first met Ken Gerberick in 1987 or '88 when I had my first solo art exhibit, at the Pitt Gallery in Vancouver. He was the curator of the show, which consisted mostly of assemblages. I took to him immediately. He also did assemblages, but his were much more adventurous and accomplished than mine.

Like me, Ken was born and raised in the States; St. Louis in his case. We also had in common a love for automobiles. Ken once told me that he remembered a car crash outside his home when he was a kid. He went out into the street and saw the smashed cars, glass, hunks of chrome and pieces of plastic spread everywhere, and he realized then and there that he wanted to do something with cars.

"One of my desires in life was to own an auto-wrecking yard; the other was to be an artist. For years I was torn between the two, then I began to combine both loves."

When Ken got to Canada, "one step ahead of the FBI" (at one point, as he fled the draft, the FBI was actually chasing him up the west coast of the U.S.), he bought a couple of acres on northern Vancouver Island, where he lived in a shack and collected junked cars and parts. He used some of the parts in assemblages but left the vehicles strewn across the property—like you'd see in the yards and hills of the Ozarks in his home state of Missouri, but more eerie because the rain forest has grabbed them in its tentacles. They are still there, merging with the surroundings.

After that first show, we traded pieces; the one Ken took from me was called "Santa Sparapartas." It was a statue of a female saint on a plinth of tires. She's leaning on an automobile bumper. Ken recognized that I was a kindred spirit.

Many years ago, Ken began to make actual automobiles into art pieces. He has created many of these rolling sculptures. The first one I saw was a black-primered 1958 Pontiac, covered with insignias from other vehicles. He eventually sold this great car to a famous punk-rock drummer, who got it on a ship back to England before the bank informed Ken that the cheque had bounced.

He had bad luck with another of his art cars, and I feel vaguely guilty about this because Ken had come to see me at my trailer in Gibsons. I wasn't at home, and when he pulled out onto Highway 101, an oblivious driver smashed into him, totalling his short.

But he has managed to accumulate a stable of transformed vehicles, which he sometimes leases out for movie productions. He has hooked up with the girl of his dreams, Janice Corrado, who shares his love and the love of refashioned automobiles.

Ken is still assembling materials and making great art out of it all. I wouldn't admit it to his face, but Mr. Gerberick is an inspiration.

U.K. FAITHFUL
Saint's remains to visit sinners, when relics tour stops at prison

Relics of a Roman Catholic saint are to stop off at Wormwood Scrubs prison as part of a visit to Britain that started this week. A casket containing bones of St. Thérèse of Lisieux, the patron saint of florists, pictured, began the one-month tour yesterday in Portsmouth and will travel on to other cities, including Leeds, Birmingham and Liverpool. The Catholic Church said crowds that have seen the relics in other countries have experienced conversion, healing, a renewed sense of vocation and the answer to their prayers. On Oct. 12, the relics of the Carmelite nun will be taken to Wormwood Scrubs prison in London, where about 25% of the prisoners are Catholic. Helen Baly, chaplain at the jail, said the casket would be placed in the prison chapel. *Reuters*

TAKE 33

AN ITEM FROM REUTERS, CLIPPED FROM THE NATIONAL POST, THURSDAY, SEPTEMBER 17, 2009—"SAINT'S REMAINS TO VISIT SINNERS, WHEN RELICS TOUR STOPS AT PRISON"

The relics of St. Thérèse of Lisieux (1873-97) had begun, the day before at Portsmouth, a one-month tour of England. Besides being slated for stops in Leeds, Birmingham and Liverpool, the relics, resting in a casket, were to be placed in the chapel at Wormwood Scrubs Prison in London.

The Reuters story doesn't give any information about Thérèse except that she was a "Carmelite nun" and the patron saint of florists. Why she is the patron of florists is not mentioned in the article. But Thérèse was known even during her lifetime as "the Little Flower of Jesus." She lived a life of small things, as she described it in her spiritual autobiography, now a classic, *L'Histoire d'une âme*.

Thérèse was only twenty-four when she died, and it was the very fact that her life was uneventful that allowed people to feel a connection with her and to project their hopes and worries onto their perception of her.

In a mystery novel, *Shanghai Alley* (1997), I have a crazed character obsessed with Thérèse.

Evidently the relics were on a world tour, because the Catholic Church press release maintained that people viewing them in other countries experienced "conversion, healing, a renewed sense of vocation and the answer to their prayers."

In art, she is often pictured with one or more roses. Her feast day is October 1.

TAKE 34

PHOTO COLLAGE: PICTURE OF ME, CUT UP AND REARRANGED

Looks better this way than did the original. I was in Saigon, had to bring a colour eight-by-ten to a movie audition. I was so disappointed or embarrassed by the result of the photograph—with my face, in other words—that I ripped the thing into about sixteen pieces. (The audition wasn't so great either.) The collage consists of eight of those pieces glued to a 4" x 5" piece of notebook paper that is painted blue.

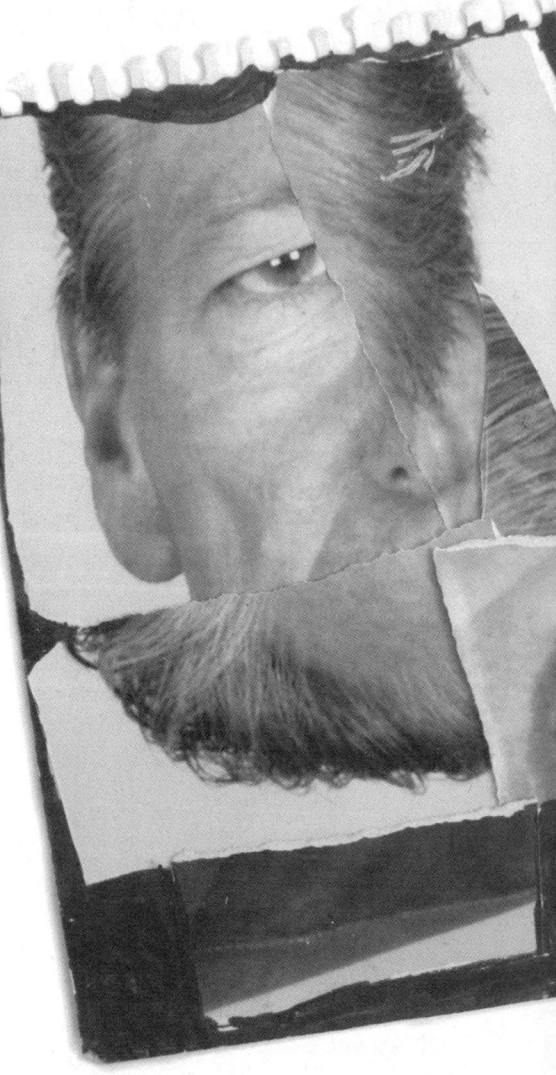

TAKE 35

A TO Z MOTORISTS' MAP OF STREETS IN CENTRAL LONDON

Price: 55p. I think I picked this up in London in 1970. It smells that old.

TAKE 36

A NOTE ON PALE YELLOW 3" X 5" INCH PAPER

"Falaise called the Killing grounds. Eisenhower Supreme Commander wrote, 'It was literally possible to walk for hundreds of yards at a time stepping on nothing but dead or decaying flesh.'"

TAKE 37

LETTER FROM AMAX NORTHWEST MINING COMPANY LIMITED, ADDRESSED TO ME ON JUNE 17, 1974, AT ROOM #107, THE EDGEWATER HOTEL, WHITEHORSE, YUKON

"We regret that we are unable to offer you the position of weather observer as advertised in the *Whitehorse Star* early in May." Etc.

Signed "R. J. R. Godfrey."

I travelled through Whitehorse innumerable times, often staying for a night or two at the Edgewater. It was the kind of place where you might be gone two years but when you walked in the desk clerk would say, "Got a letter for you."

I wonder what became of Mr. Godfrey.

TAKE 38

HALF OF A BLACK-AND-WHITE PHOTOGRAPH THAT HAS BEEN SCISSORED VERTICALLY

It shows a man in a light-coloured uniform holding the door of a limousine, probably a Rolls Royce, open with his left, black-gloved hand. He's wearing a cap that matches the uniform. In the glass of the opened window, you can see part of the right side of another man in a business suit; his neck also visible before his jaw vanishes in the dark. The man has a high white collar and appears to be holding a bundle, also white, in his bent right arm. The chauffeur looks like he wants to smile but is not going to commit himself to the photographer for fear of offending some important person.

On the other side of the half-photograph, written in green ink, is the note "Myself in flying uniform in England 1951."

I met this man in a bar in Toronto in the late '70s. He told me that after the war, he worked as a chauffeur before coming to Canada. I seem to recall we became great friends for a few hours and he spoke freely. I never saw or heard from him again but I remember his last name was Smith.

TAKE 39

"THOUGHT DU JOUR"

From the *Globe and Mail*:

"School is an institution built on the axiom that learning is the result of teaching. And institutional wisdom continues to accept this axiom, despite overwhelming evidence to the contrary."
—Ivan Illich

TAKE 40

TRAIN TICKET ISSUED BY TRANZ SCENIC, TRANZ RAIL LIMITED OF WELLINGTON, NEW ZEALAND

I note that the railway offices are on Bunny Street.

Anyway, the train trip is actually known as the Trans Alpine. It's one of the great railway journeys, from Greymouth to Christchurch on the South Island. Although it only covers about 325 kilometres, it goes from the wild Indian Ocean coast over the Southern Alps to emerge on the Canterbury Plain. Unlike other great rail trips (the Indian-Pacific, for instance, in Australia), this train carries locals.

And one of the stops along the way, in the mountains, is the focus for one of the world's great dog stories. I had heard that there was a mutt—name of Rosie—who met the train every day and was given a meat pie by the conductor. The dog had started doing this one day for no apparent reason. Its owner never reminded it of the train's imminent arrival; it just knew the timetable. As we were nearing the town, the conductor announced that of late, the dog had been missing trips, due to age and illness. I was quite disappointed at the announcement. In Auckland, I had mentioned the story to friends, and they had teased me for believing anything so far-fetched. I could just hear them asking me when I got back if I had seen the little doggie. But, the conductor continued, awhile back the dog had taken on a protégé who sometimes filled in for it. And so it was when a young brown mutt came racing through the crowd on the platform to get its meat pie.

TAKE 41

AN ACCORDION-TYPE, FOLD-OUT PAMPHLET, ACCOMPANYING A SHOW AT THE NATIONAL GALLERY OF CANADA THAT RAN FROM 30 MARCH TO 21 MAY 1990, CONSISTING OF WORKS BY JAMES WILSON MORRICE (1865–1924), FROM THE G. BLAIR LAING COLLECTION

I like Morrice's paintings and went to Ottawa to see the show. The writing in the pamphlet cracks me up. This kind of stuff has been going on as long as Canadian writers have been commenting on Canadian art. It seems the criticism has gone from stuffy old dullness to post-modern gibberish. As soon as I read the following bit, I wanted to quote it and was relieved not to see the author's name. But on the last folded section, I found his name in small print. Alas, I am duty bound to state that the responsible party is Charles C. Hill, "Curator of Canadian Art."

Mr. Hill writes of Morrice, "His life was uneventful and is best summed up in the text published in the catalogue of the small retrospective exhibition accorded him in the 1924 Salon d'Automne:

> Few lives have been as impenetrable as that of this nostalgic Canadian. At the Quai des Grands-Augustins, then at the Quai de la Tournelle, he was always surrounded by trunks, ready to leave on trains and steamships. Born in Montreal, he enjoyed living in Paris or on the coast of Brittany, between Concerneau and Le Pouldu. However, he would suddenly pack his bags and set out for Spain, Italy, Algeria, or Morocco. He would resurface at his Paris residence, then disappear again, sending to the Salon d'Automne paintings he had done in Jamaica or Cuba. A very cultivated man—he was qualified to practice law in Canada—he would only lay down his brushes to pick up a book. Montaigne, Baudelaire, Verlaine. His father left him a very large fortune some ten years ago, allowing him to give himself up completely to the fantasies of his dream and of his art.

Yes, that certainly illustrates that Morrice led an uneventful life. In the pamphlet there is a Karsh photograph of G. Blair Laing, who has a good face, very human.

TAKE 42

JOHN MONTGOMERY ITEMS: ONE LETTER, A PHOTOGRAPH, ONE NEWSPAPER ARTICLE (BY ME), ONE POEM (BY HIM)

In the late '70s, I wrote an essay about Jack Kerouac that appeared in the *Globe and Mail*. The piece was occasioned by the posthumous publication of Kerouac's *Visions of Cody*. The *Globe*'s book editor, Ed O'Dacre, told me that he was taking quite a chance by assigning me the piece. And he was. The book world then was nearly as conservative as it is now—at least in Canada—and Kerouac was considered a joke, an author for adolescents and literary retards.

Not long after the essay was published, I got a letter from a man named John Montgomery, who lived in California. He had read and liked my piece, and announced that he was the model for Henry Morley in *Dharma Bums*, and had appeared as Couglin and Fairbrother in other Kerouac novels, particularly *Desolation Angels* and *Satori in Paris*. The way he described himself subsequently was as a bit-part actor in "roles for Jack Kerouac bookmovie Eisenstein impresario of the Dulouz legend."

He is the third man, along with Kerouac and Gary Snyder (Japhy Ryder), in that legendary attempt at climbing the California Matterhorn. Montgomery or "Morley" is the one who has to hike back down before they reach the summit because he has forgotten to drain the radiator of his Ford Zephyr. Kerouac, no mechanic or car driver, either, for that matter, calls the radiator the "carburetor." Anyway, as Montgomery, the only mountaineer of the bunch, had nothing to prove, it didn't matter if he completed the climb.

I answered Montgomery's letter; he wrote back immediately, and we were launched on a correspondence that lasted until his death nearly twenty years later. Shortly after that initial exchange, a large cardboard box was delivered to the place where I was living on Howland Avenue in Toronto. I remember it so distinctly because my brother was there, and after opening the box, which was three feet tall, we stared all befuddled at the contents. Inside were ridiculous ties, a couple of pairs of argyle socks, a three-week-old copy of the *San Francisco Chronicle*, some oatmeal chocolate chip cookies (stale) and a book about the inland sea in Japan (that I still have). It was from Montgomery. After John died, a publisher in the States did a tribute anthology; my essay in that book wasn't the only one to note his penchant for improbable gifts. I think it was Allen Ginsberg who wrote about Montgomery showing up at a party, bringing as his contribution to the affair a colonial-style chair missing one leg.

The thing is, Montgomery was not trying to be unconventional or kooky. He was completely natural. And he was one of the great talkers, though sometimes you didn't know what the hell he was talking about; actually, most of the time you wouldn't know what the hell he was talking about. But something he said would stick in your mind, and three weeks or three years later, you'd suddenly get it. He could get Lawrence of Arabia, Anwar Sadat, Howard Hughes and Carol Doda into the same sentence, and while you were trying to figure that out, he'd ask, "You know where I might unload a few Sinkiewicz first editions?"

Here is a letter from him, undated, on a half-sheet of green paper. Since he typed it in italics, I will render it thus:

Dear Jim,

We are having a winter drought-record making, SF Bay Area. It is at times cold though.

The press seems to be giving an all-out excoriation of Ronald Reagan. I don't watch TV so I don't know how much of this is also done there. The Demo tide is turning to Mondale.

I saw most of the State of the Union speech which was rhetorical.

The young Mex. Army Sgt. Grenada hero who appeared by request of R. Reagan seemed embarrassed by the applause although he played it cool.

I continue a mild comedy of errors, two dental students working independently renovating my oral cavity, saving me money and losing me sick leave time but also work boredom. It all takes place at the dental school at Univ Calif center, a 1980 4-story bldg.

I've discovered a mountaineering poet, Edwin Brummond, British, now in SF; I think climbs Yosemite walls and SF bldgs. Wife climbs. Haven't met them yet. He sent me gratis 1st class a privately pub. Paperbound of his poems. The best one I've read of them is of a visit to the Dentist.

Got a visit from a woman, Sierra Club, mountain peak climber (hiking type), it encourages her collecting instinct. She teaches English to orientals in the L.A. schools. Came thru here after I wrote her, obtaining her name from a no. of sheets of "Single booklovers" given me by an old Commie friend who did so as he had found a woman. They're both retired; and he suffered loneliness. He paints and is poor at it but it gives him kicks or therapy.

He recently gave me a coffee table some one had thrown out. They both collect castoffs and abandoned things; it (the commonalty) interferes with Sol's competitive instinct. He is an oddball Jew.

Toronto has become a hot used book collecting town according to the Globe & Mail. I have a Kerouac penpal who travels Arnprior-Ottawa-Toronto weekly with his wife. I guess they shop & get kulchured up. She is an MD and I think he is a househusband. One baby and another due. I guess Medicos are better paid than U.S. ones.

I have a new AXE HANDLES, poems by Snyder to sell at 40 off if Snyder's sister doesn't need it. Snyder gets more sedate. Cute cover, colors and a kind of childish goddess figure done by a Japanese who lives at Green Gulch, Marin headlands Zen center. The Zen they practice must be highly alien to Japan. The big Zen centers in Hawaii are both run by Robert Aitken so you be the judge. Hawaii has lotsa Koreans too. Annyonghi gassipsio is goodbye in that language.

The Sierra Club woman is sharing an apt. nonsex with a young Filipino man she met as he was her student. The woman seems quite hung up.

                 Over

2) This letter is turning out to be a kind of Melting Pot Meld tale. In spite of all, I continue saving money. I recently lost a bit as I tried to twist out my radiator petcock and they are welded in the model Ford I have and it paid to have the dealer take it out and send it out. The dealers shops aren't much now. This a large SF dealer too.

My overall plan is to pay off mortgage in summer. Also, I have a date I hope to climb in the Palisades, a Sierra Club trip over 4 cols with 3 peaks' possibility (non-roped). I have written a letter of inquiry. The dates are August 6-13. Price 155.00. 2 layover days during which 3 peaks can be climbed; I haven't the detailed sheet on it as yet—probably Split Mtn, Middle Palisade & North Palisade. Split is otherwise South Palisade. These are relatively steep and I suppose climbed along the "arêtes" or from the ends, possibly S. I have the appropriate Climber's Guide. I think they now have it separated between climber & mountaineer the Club meaning that non-rope climbers are mountaineers. At any rate, it (the area) is in from Big Pine, above (N) of Lone Pine & Independence I think. You drive up to 1 or the other then prob. go around S to N, into Dusy Basin & back next to Thunderbolt Peak (a harder slightly smaller generally steeper peak) that is over a col & over to a small bldg. at 4th Lake then by trail back to Big Pine Lodge. I would rather go with a smaller non "Club" group but don't know enough people.

You're welcome to come along; they might restrict to Club members—it is such a large club now—I don't know how large but many belong out of political conservationist reasons.

I went through W to E on trail going out past Mt. Still & Agassiz Needle (N of the Palisades). The Needle is not a needle it's a misnomer. Then I went over a col S. of Split I think going E to W, broke my glasses, lost my pack, swam the Middle Fork of the Kings and got out o.k., using food stored in a cabin I found.

    So I dislike solo trips really. They now charge 6.00 per car per nite to use a Forest Camp of the improved type. They have all nite lights in the toilets, large mirrors, unglazed tile on the inside walls, and God knows what.

    Yosemite Park—the Valley has an act with a man impersonating Muir (certain dates I guess or maybe he has a job there). A Conversation with a Tramp I think it's called. They give kids junior ranger badges for collecting 2 certificates for picking up litter (I think). I would like to go there with a kid and make a deal to buy his badge to add to my Eagle Scout pin.

    I went to funeral of mother of ex-wife No.2 (the multiple sclerosis case, a special deal). The minister for that was also there when my daughter was a Sunday School teacher. Unitarians. I never would have encouraged that. Her mother was raised a Catholic more or less at father's behest. Her mother in turn was a Protestant—the couple each attended its church all their lives. The father's father threw him out for marrying a non-Cath. Or at least refused to allow the wife in the house. All in N.Y. City.
I ran out of paper, but as Kerouac said, keep on truckin.

    John

Soon after we began corresponding, Montgomery invited me to come and visit, but it was a couple of years before I was able to get down there. I got my Canadian citizenship in 1974, about the time we started writing, but I wasn't keen on visiting the U.S. of A. I guess it was in 1976 that I met him for the first time. He was living in a fourplex apartment unit in Palo Alto. He had told me to come at night, which I did, but he hadn't told me how late at night. It was after midnight when he showed up from his shift at the post office. I was waiting outside the front door of the building. When I announced myself, he just mumbled, "Hhhmmm," opened the door of the apartment and immediately vanished into another room. I sat for half an hour, reading the titles of books on his shelves. When he finally emerged, it was in mid-sentence: "because Jack warned me to stay away from him. Neal, he said, was a hedonist; but was always nice and friendly. Best liked man in Bohemia. First time I saw Cassady, he was wearing jeans and a denim jacket, which just wasn't seen in those days. Looked like a cowboy on loan from Central Casting. Another thing.............."

Montgomery had the highest IQ ever tested at the University of California at Berkeley, yet knowing he could never adjust to an academic life, he never tried. Of his many degrees, two were in Library Science, and he worked at that in various states but was forever harassing library users, lecturing them on their fields of interest. Ask him for a book on hieroglyphics, you'd get a discourse. Better the students should have just taken notes on what he said. Anyway, he finally quit libraries to drive a cab in San Francisco. When I asked him if he'd ever driven any famous people, he replied, "I had Spike Jones and Lucius Beebe. But not at the same time."

In fact, one could never get a straight answer out of John. Kerouac couldn't; I couldn't; no one else could either. He was born sometime between 1922 and 1925, either in Oregon, California or Washington. I knew he spent time as a kid in Stockton. When I asked him what that was like, he told me "It had the first Filipino labour union in the United States."

His conversation was like a mad river and sought its own channels. If you inquired about the atmosphere at the famous Six Gallery event in 1956, which he attended, when Ginsberg first read "Howl," with Rexroth officiating, Kerouac passing the wine jug and Cassady shouting encouragement, John would diverge into the intricacies of Farsi.

One time, I visited him in San Anselmo, and he offered to pay me to break up his concrete parking pad and cart the chunks away. The work was difficult but would have been pleasant enough but for John making it complicated with his opinions, advice and questions. I recalled that he had once hired Kerouac to help him dig out a basement in Berkeley. Kerouac wrote about that experience in *Desolation Angels*. When the work was over, Kerouac vowed never to work for another person ever again in his life. When I was done with John's parking pad, I made the same vow. Kerouac was able to keep his vow, but—alas—I wasn't.

The photograph in the Sweet Assorted box is black and white, and shows John Montgomery and Robert Frank. The photographer and filmmaker is wearing a flannel shirt that looks like it might have been handed down from Kerouac, who wrote the introduction to Frank's book of photographs, *The Americans*. He is pictured full face, and it's a mischievous face; his head is bare to the crown, and his hair reminds me of Curly of the three stooges. Frank has a full lower lip and big eyes, which are looking to his left. Montgomery is uncharacteristically duded up, in a black tuxedo of all things and in his left hand, he's holding a half-full glass of white wine, even though he didn't drink. The forefinger of the hand holding the glass seems to be pointing vaguely in the direction that Frank is looking. Montgomery might be indicating something going on across the room—maybe he's making a satirical comment about someone; Frank looks like he's contemplating going over there and goosing the person.

Here is the last John Montgomery item. It's a poem by him, in italic script, titled *No Higher Octane:*

*In the central casting parking lot where Adam
Found internal combustion, the self-starter
Was promised to him foretelling eternal
                    Locomotion to come.
Even now in the ruins of Twentieth Century Fox
Maids and slaveys tool about in vintage Cadillacs
A memory of that saintly paddler who searched
For the last Fleetwood canoes too soon*

*In those mobilehomes away from home
The stars' dressingrooms with God-given per diem
There is belief in the infinite mileage
Of Benevolent Mother of Shirl Temples, She
Who conceived plots and business immaculately.
The God-giver well remembered with compass,
Cross, crescent wrench, beads.*

*The entourage a miracle away, surrounded
By its heavenly host of multimedia designers
Writing in neat director's chairs a portent
Of salvation; a coating of True Simonize
Which will never wash off; waiting since Buster Keaton
For a Block Buster Preview.*

*An emanation of a silver Ghost Rolls Royce,
One never before seen by man;
Never viewed by Consumers' Union
            Under floodlights
                    Descending from the chauffeur seat*

                Messiah Mark II

Looking perhaps strangely like Redford

> His honor guard of outriders
> Ford   Damier   Renault   Ferrari
> The four shining horsepowermen

> A Fiat Lux under floodlights

> The endless penitential effort
> Of America's ten thousand car wash machines

> Purification justified regardless of emission

> A little virgin Jeep, undercoating barely dry
> Leading the way to Apocalypse.

Apropos of driving, that is one area where John Montgomery was not very accomplished. In fact, to put it bluntly, he couldn't drive for shit. One time he was driving Ginsberg up Mount Tamalpais, and Ginsberg vocalized his fear at the way Montgomery negotiated the mountain road. "But you're not afraid of heroin," Montgomery said.

"That's not as dangerous," was Ginsberg's reply.

I was in the passenger's seat one day, when John went through a stop sign and ran into the curb on the other side of the intersection. When I said something on the order of, "Jesus, John!" he asked, "What?"

I trepidatiously suggested that he might give a little more attention to the task at hand, in his hands, which was getting to the store and back without harm. Genuinely perplexed, he said, "But Kerouac told me I was the greatest driver he'd ever met, next to Neal."

"He was only kidding you, John."

Once I showed up on time at our appointed meeting place, outside a cigar store in San Francisco. John was posed arms folded, blanket over his shoulders, next to the wooden Indian.

One time he drove up to Vancouver to stay at my Comox Street apartment for a few days. He'd paid for his gas on the trip up by selling drama books at used-book stores. My friend Joe Ferone and I got a ride south as far as Bend, Oregon. John commented on everything along the way, flora, fauna, humans and architecture. He knew that 19th century secretaries of state and obscure women novelists had been born here or there. We convinced him to keep to back roads since his speed never exceeded 40 miles an hour.

One time he saw me off at the bus in San Francisco for the trip to Vancouver. When it was ready to pull out, his face creased into a smile and he did a little jig, clasped me awkwardly by the shoulders and turned and walked off mumbling, all quick as a wink.

I called after him, "See you, John." But he didn't reply.

Later, I found this line in *Desolation Angels*, where he and Kerouac were parting, "'Well, so long Henry'—and he didn't answer but just walked off shrugging."

I was living in Peachland, B.C., in 1992, when I learned that he had died. He had just come down from the mountain and had a heart attack.

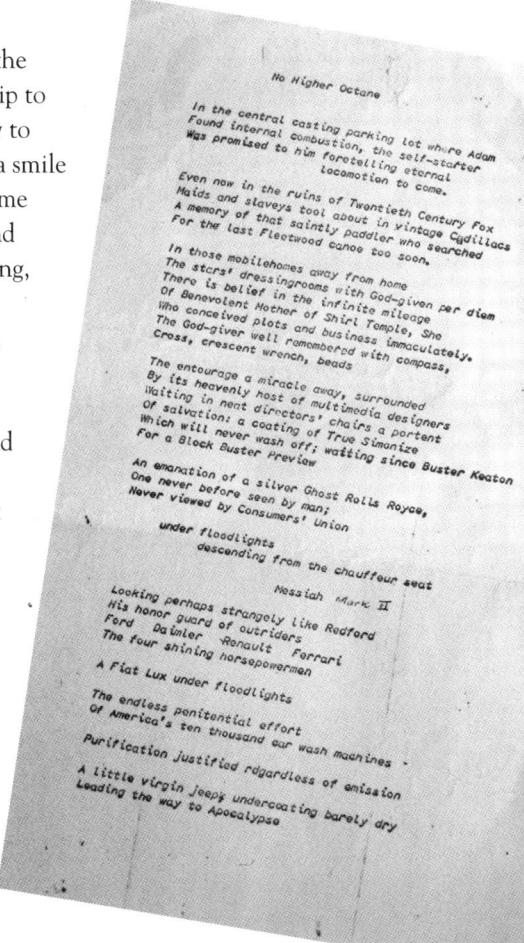

No Higher Octane

In the central casting parking lot where Adam
Found internal combustion, the self-starter
Was promised to him foretelling eternal
                                locomotion to come.

Even now in the ruins of Twentieth Century Fox
Maids and slaveys tool about in vintage Cadillacs
A memory of that saintly paddler who searched
For the last Fleetwood canoe too soon.

In those mobilehomes away from home
The stars' dressingrooms with God-given per diem
There is belief in the infinite mileage
Of Benevolent Mother of Shirl Temple, She
Who conceived plots and business immaculately.
The God-giver well remembered with compass,
Cross, crescent wrench, beads

The entourage a miracle away, surrounded
By its heavenly host of multimedia designers
Waiting in neat directors' chairs a portent
Of salvation: a coating of True Simonize
Which will never wash off; waiting since Buster Keaton
For a Block Buster Preview

An emanation of a silver Ghost Rolls Royce,
One never before seen by man;
Never viewed by Consumers' Union

under floodlights
        descending from the chauffeur seat

                                Messiah Mark II
Looking perhaps strangely like Redford
His honor guard of outriders
Ford   Daimler   Renault   Ferrari
The four shining horsepowermen

A Fiat Lux under floodlights

The endless penitential effort
Of America's ten thousand car wash machines
Purification justified regardless of emission

A little virgin jeeps undercoating barely dry
Leading the way to Apocalypse

TAKE 43

TWO PHOTOGRAPHS

One picture, faded colour, was taken in Baton Rouge, Louisiana; the date the photo was developed was "Sep 67."

I took the picture at a July 4th patriot parade. It shows a soldier standing in an open trailer being pulled by a jeep. He has his battle helmet on, left foot lifted and resting on the lip of the trailer, and he's holding his bayoneted rifle. There are other jeeps visible. I remember that parade, the show of military hardware and the hostile looks we got—my friends and I—from the locals. It was the summer of love, and we were on our way to San Francisco. We had to depart from Baton Rouge because the patriots began moving in on us.

The owner of the finned Plymouth that we travelled in across country, down into Mexico and back, is the subject of the black-

and-white photograph that is dated "Jul 68." His name was Ed Vogel. He's wearing a flannel shirt and sandals and lying on his side on the roof of my apartment building on Eldridge Street, near Grand and Bowery, in New York City. He has his left hand in a paper bag. Maybe he's going to bring out a can of beer. I hope so.

> DON'T GET SENT TO VIETNAM
> We can help you fight the draft
> You Are Not Alone!
> Youth Against War & Fascism
> 58 West 25th Street, N. Y. C.
> 242-9225 WW-46 W, 21 st St. 675-2520
> Draft Counselling
> & Legal Referral Available

We had met at West Chester College in Chester County, Pennsylvania. He was a clean-cut, conservative music student when I first saw him, but within a short time he became a left-winger, eventually joining a group called Youth Against War and Fascism. Their card gave their address at 58 West 25th Street in New York and bore the legend:

DON'T GET SENT TO VIETNAM

We can help you fight the draft

You Are Not Alone!

In April, 1968, Ed and I took a harrowing trip from NYC headed for Atlanta, Georgia, and the funeral of Martin Luther King. We had been attending a lecture by Herbert Aptheker at a union hall on the lower east side when it was announced that King had been murdered. Ed and I made our way down and back along the east coast of an America in flames.

In Baltimore, the cops had been just about to sic the German shepherd on us when we were saved by sniper fire. We'd managed to get on a special bus on the outskirts that went into the centre of the city. At the Greyhound station, we had to get special passes that enabled us to walk the three blocks to the Trailways station, where a bus would take us near where we wanted to go in Pennsylvania.

There was no one but police in those three blocks. We were hassled by all, but the ones with the dog were the worst. The cops were taunting us, and the dog, encouraged by them, was red-eyed, teeth bared, and dripping saliva. The cops laughed, but their laughs ended when someone fired at them from the third floor of a building across the way. Ed and I hit the pavement, rolled to the curb, and lay there protected by an automobile. After what seemed like half an hour but was probably one, two or three minutes, the shooting stopped, and the cops rushed toward the building. Ed and I got up, brushed ourselves off and hurried on our way.

We never got to Atlanta, being jailed in Weldon, North Carolina; the sheriff held us until he was sure there was no possible way we could get to "Martin Luther Coon's" funeral.

On red ink on the backs of both photos are prison-censor's stamps. I had sent the photos to the friend incarcerated in the middle west who, in my "novella" *Real Gone*, I call "Val Santee." He has signed and numbered the photos.

After moving to Canada in October 1968, I had no contact with Ed Vogel, though I've often wondered what happened to him. I did see him once. It was in 1976, during my first trip back to the United States. I was in New York and stopped into a Chock Full of Nuts for lunch. They had these winding counters that reminded me of rivers doubling back on themselves. Two men in suits sat down across a bend in the river from me. One of them was Ed Vogel. I couldn't hear what they were saying, but from the looks of them, the subject wasn't radical politics. I didn't speak to him. Ed was obviously on a different path now, and I wouldn't have wanted to embarrass him before his associates.

TAKE 44

SHORT NOTE, CLIPPED FROM A NEWSPAPER

"The Sedlec Ossuary, a church near Kutna Hora in the Czech Republic, is decorated with human bones, including an elaborate chandelier made entirely from skeletal remains. (www.kirchersociety.org)"

TAKE 45

MAROON-COLOURED MATCHBOOK, ADVERTISING ESTAY'S SEAFOOD RESTAURANT, "HOME OF THE TOPLESS OYSTERS"

There are two burnt matches left in the book. On the inner spine is "CRAWFISH, CRABS, and SHRIMP." The "Owner and Operator" is Wallace G. Fedora, telephone number: (504) 395-7077.

I like the matchbook, the colour of it, and like to think that ESTAY'S was a salubrious joint. I regret not calling there because I was and am curious as to whether the owner and operator is related to the original designer of the hat by the same name.

TAKE 46

SKETCH IN BLUE INK FOR A SCULPTURE OR ASSEMBLAGE THAT I INTENDED TO MAKE BUT NEVER DID

It still looks like a good idea. Different pieces of wood, shaped and painted; assembled to present some sort of abstraction of a creature; looks like it has horns and a sort of trunk.

On the back of this sketch torn from an art pad is the number for a tube of acrylic paint: "Aquatech 48474 A/H 83914 82485."

Underneath those numbers is a squiggly line and the sentence: "Chipboard mill next door to Taupo Native Plant were dumping black ___ into nursery."

Taupo is in New Zealand. I've been there a few times but don't remember when this was written.

TAKE 47

PIECE OF PAPER TORN FROM A HOTEL TELEPHONE PAD

The hotel is the Moctezuma in the section of Mexico City of the same name. A good place, half an hour from the airport. I've stayed there several times, mainly when it has been necessary to wait overnight to catch an ongoing flight in Mexico; to Oaxaca, for instance. A couple of streets from the hotel, some people operate a hot auto-parts racket. Customers call a secret number with their wants, and a time is arranged for the pickup. Car pulls up, guy rushes from a doorway or from behind a fence, takes the driver's money, hands him the crankshaft and both disappear. The transaction never takes more than a minute.

Anyway, I must have been angry at the political situation—which means the note could have been written any day or every day. What was particularly annoying me this day were affluent middle-class lefties, which reminds me of some right-wing politician's definition of a left-winger, as "someone who is two steps to the left on any given issue until it affects him personally."

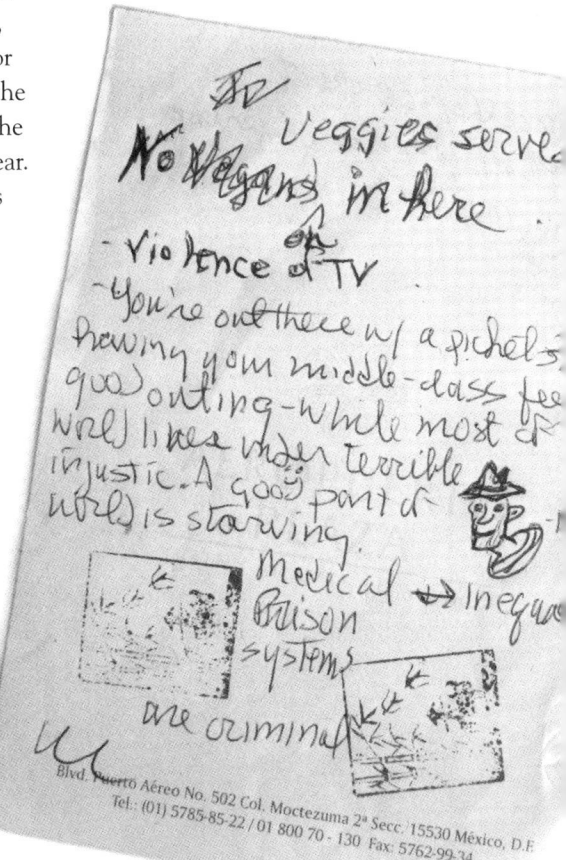

89

So I made a few points; perhaps I intended to write something. One thing I intended to comment on is violence on TV. Then I wrote, "You're out there w/a picket sign having your middle-class, feel-good outing while most of the world lives under terrible injustice. A good part of the world is starving." After that, I note, "Medical inequalities, prison systems are criminal."

I also have a line, "No veggies served in here." I hate the term "veggies." I don't know why and I'm sure it's irrational. So sue me.

One time in Hanoi, I had a wooden stamp made. It pictures bamboo, a river and a boat. I bought a stamp pad with blue ink. I gave it to my stepson on his birthday. He looked at it contemptuously, put it down on a table and never picked it up again. I kept it. I used it to stamp twice on this piece of telephone-pad paper. Why I took it on a trip to Mexico, I don't know.

On the other side of the paper, I wrote, "politically correct. M.A. in Salt Spring." So to add to my political screed, I was going to write about political correctness. I was reminding myself to mention Mary Anne—who I mention in the part about St. Augustine. We were living on Salt Spring Island in the summer of 1982. She had taken the ferry to Victoria to apply for a job. As she was leaving the boat on her return, a local Salt Spring woman—a typical, well-off dowdy New Ager—felt it incumbent upon herself to deliver a lecture. She criticized Mary Anne for the way she was attired: dress, stockings, heels. Told her it was ignorant and helped to perpetuate stereotypes. She never asked Mary Anne why she was dressed that way or where she had been. Of course, the woman herself didn't work—didn't have to.

One time on Salt Spring, I picked up a New Ager who was hitchhiking. He was in his late forties, had thinning hair halfway down his back, and was carrying a package, two-and-a-half feet high and wrapped in brown paper, from the post office. He unwrapped the package and took out the contents: a $700 juicer. No sooner was he finished raving about all the things he could do with turnips and oranges than he began to tell me how out of it I was for driving such a hog of an automobile. It was a '67 Chrysler that I bought for $35 from a farmer on the island. When I went to look at it, there were chickens living in the trunk. Well, I let the guy continue with his rant about the gas-guzzling monster and how I was supporting the oil companies. At the first pull-out, I stopped and made him get out.

Another note I made is "dating contracts." I had just read that in many U.S. universities, it was required that males sign papers on which are written their intentions during the course of dates. These must be presented to the females. This sounds like the premise for a potentially hilarious stand-up routine, but alas, it was serious. The thing is, how does one know what one is going to do? Do you write, "Clause three: After smoking the second joint, I intend to bend her forward over the arm of the couch and…" But what if you state your intention to kiss her after the first glass of wine but find you have absolutely no desire to do so? Have you broken the contract? Can she take you to court?

How come all these people who are so dedicated to making rules and regulations consider themselves to be left-wingers? And can this absolute inability to comprehend the real world—this total alienation—have anything to do with the fact that the left in North America has been moribund since the 1930s?

TAKE 48

PRESS PASS FOR ATTENDANCE AT EXPO '86 IN VANCOUVER

My position is given as "reporter"; my employer, the "*Village Voice.*" It's a red-and-white card with my photo. I was hired by the famous NYC weekly to cover Expo from a different viewpoint than other organs. I worked for a couple of days, and then my three-storey apartment building caught on fire. The flames began in the front stairwell. My apartment was the only one between the front windows and the front stairwell. Everyone else got out through the back stairwell. Me, I shrugged and jumped from my third-floor window. I thought it would not be a problem. I broke my ankle and was thus unable to complete my assignment for the *Village Voice*.

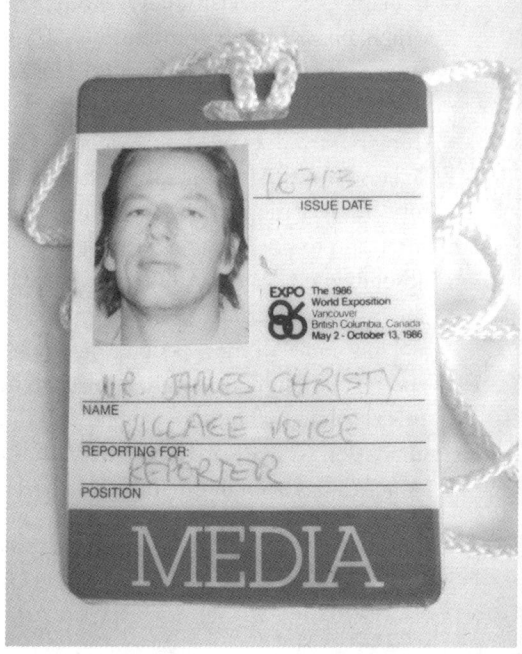

I did, however, get a telephone call from entrepreneur and Expo organizer Jimmy Pattison one night in response to my call. We talked for an hour and a half; I was amazed that he could spare the time. I later gave him a bit part as a nine-year-old trumpet-playing kid in my novel *Shanghai Alley*. He had been a nine-year-old trumpet-playing kid.

TAKE 49

A KENNEDY HALF-DOLLAR

I forgot I had this. I despise John F. Kennedy, a charlatan and the man who got America involved in the Vietnam War, which marked the beginning of the decline of that empire. His father made a deal with the mob. They would deliver West Virginia and Chicago; in exchange there would be no Justice Department investigation of organized crime. The mob lived up to their part of the deal; Kennedy didn't and paid the consequences. He was upstairs sexing Angie Dickinson the night he was inaugurated while his wife sat at the dinner table next to his empty chair. When asked how it had been, Ms. Dickinson replied, "In a sense, it was the best twenty seconds of my life."

Other girlfriends were kinder, dubbing him, "The one-minute man."

And what a sophisticated statesman! Who can forget his famous speech in Berlin when he said, "I, too, am a jelly doughnut."

So if you want this silver half dollar, drop me a line (care of the publisher).

TAKE 50

INDICTMENT

THE GRAND JURY CHARGES:

That on or about April 7, 1969, and continuing from day to day thereafter, in Lansdowne, in the Eastern District of Pennsylvania, JAMES RICHARD CHRISTY, being a male person subject to the rules and regulations of the Military Selective Service Act of 1967 and the rules and regulations made pursuant thereto, did knowingly and unlawfully fail, neglect and refuse to perform a duty required of him by the provisions of the said Act, in that he did knowing fail, neglect and refuse to comply with a valid and lawful order of Local Board 58, Fidelity-Lansdowne Bldg., Lansdowne and Baltimore Avenues, Lansdowne, Pa. 19050, dated March 19, 1969, directing him to report for and submit to induction into the Armed Forces of the United States, on April 7, 1969.

In violation of 50 Appendix, U.S.C. S 462.

A TRUE BILL

(signed)

By which time, I was already happily ensconced in Toronto, Canada, and made no response. I had failed to report at other times and even mailed them my draft. One time I did report and was the only one who did not take that step forward to be inducted. They held me until a lawyer got me out of detention with some hocus pocus and bafflegab.

It never occurred to me to go into the Armed Services. I kick myself for waiting so long to make up my mind about coming to Canada. I exhausted all other options that I shouldn't even have considered: applying for conscientious-objector status, going to Sweden, changing my identity. (I could have done the latter but didn't as I no longer had the slightest interest in being an American.)

TAKE 51

CLIPPING FROM A NEW ZEALAND NEWSPAPER, FROM SOMETIME IN 1989. THE HEADLINE IS, "AVANT-GARDE PLAN ON OFFER TO CAPITAL."

I admire the artist and architect Frederick Hundertwasser. He abhorred the straight line and hated the ice-cube trays and cigarette lighters that make up modern architecture, as well as all the little houses laid out on streets that resemble the inside of a waffle iron.

I clipped the article from an Auckland newspaper on my first trip to New Zealand in 1989. Here's the first paragraph:

"… Frederick Hundertwasser battled for years to be the designer of an unconventional apartment building in Vienna which now attracts some 2000 tourists a day."

I've never seen this apartment building, unfortunately. One of the results of its unlikely success is that Hundertwasser got to design many other buildings throughout the world. They feature wavy floors and rooflines, gardens on the roofs, windows at odd angles, and often use recycled material in the construction. Hundertwasser was often around the building site, consulting with the tradesmen; in fact, he usually gave them the responsibility of doing the job how they best saw fit.

In the '70s, he sailed his reworked cargo ship from Vienna to New Zealand, bought land on the North Island and became a naturalized citizen. He was known locally around Kawakawa for planting 50,000 trees on his property. He maintained other homes: a villa in Venice and a house in Normandy. The article that I clipped calls him "one of the world's most highly paid artists."

Hundertwasser designed a building which he offered to the city of Wellington, New Zealand's capital, which would "symbolize the bridging of Maori and European cultures" and would contain archives, a museum, a theatre, conference rooms, offices and restaurants.

His building had enthusiastic support from Wellington's mayor at the time, Jim Belich, who said, "Here we have a world-renowned figure—already a legend in his own time—offering us something for nothing out of the goodness of his heart… Because of the special skills of this man and his background, the offer is something that should not be passed over lightly."

It was.

More conventional, less adventurous minds prevailed. Hundertwasser also designed a new flag for New Zealand, featuring a green koru, the fern native to the country. That was passed over too.

But he did get one project completed in New Zealand before his death in 2000. It was in the town of Kawakawa. I visited there on the first New Zealand trip, finding it a moribund little place, a dried-up mining town. Absolutely nothing happening on a sunny Saturday afternoon.

Hundertwasser was granted the right to build public toilets on the main street. One can only imagine the hassle he went through to get the idea approved. Public toilets for whom? There was never any public on the streets. Hundertwasser enlisted locals to take part. They brought him used bottles, old tiles and other cast-off products. The result is a colourful little building that can't help but make a visitor smile.

On my second trip to Kawakawa, in 2004, the town had been revived. Shops had been opened near the toilets, and some of the proprietors had imitated Hundertwasser in their decorations. I called again in 2008, and this time Kawakawa was actually crowded, with new businesses catering to the many visitors. I stayed in the nearby beach town of Opua, and on a walk discovered that kids from the local elementary school had gone to Kawakawa on a field trip and become so excited by Hundertwasser's building that they wanted to do something similar. The result was that the school, with wisdom rarely, if ever, displayed by educators, allowed them to do just that. A couple of workers put up the shells of playhouses and domes and poles, and the kids were left on their own to decorate them. Quite a legacy Mr. Hundertwasser left.

TAKE 52

**ONE PHOTOGRAPH FROM BUENOS AIRES;
TWO FROM SAIGON**

I'm in the habit of visiting second-hand stores and flea markets, especially in foreign countries, and looking for old photographs and curious items—such as the Italian print of a scene from the walls of Pompeii that I bought for next to nothing in Trinidad while covering the Lalonde-Stewart fight and staying at the upside-down hotel (Take 20). Anyway, two photos are from two different shops in Saigon; the other, from a flea market in Buenos Aires.

    The one from Buenos Aires shows a dapper man with slicked-back hair standing by an automobile from the early '30s; he has one hand in the pocket of his tan-coloured suit (I'm assuming it is tan; the photo is black and white). The other hand, his right, is pressed against the car near where a side-view mirror might be. Maybe there is a side-view mirror and his hand is covering it, but one can't be sure, because the bottom border of the photo cuts across his hand. There is, however, plenty of sky at the top of the picture. There are trees in the background, a building beyond the automobile and on the right side of the photograph.

The tango would have been going strong then, and Carlos Gardel would have been at his peak. Gardel was the heart and soul of the tango, just as tango is the heart and soul of Buenos Aires. It mattered not that he was born in Toulouse, France. Argentina mourned when he was killed in a plane crash at age forty.

One of the Saigon photos shows a young man with a hairstyle that would become popular in the next decade in America. In fact, the kid looks like he could be a dark-complexioned prototype for a young rockabilly sensation. Good-looking, with a sort of half-smile. On the back is the date 2-9-48. Vietnamese characters run down the left and right margins.

The other shows two stylish women (they're both in their late twenties): one looks French; the other could be, too, but could also be part French, part Vietnamese. They are walking along a sunny street in the afternoon (I know the street they're walking along), late '50s, probably—before the Americans admitted they were in the country. They are both wearing shades and sandals with straps wound to above the ankles. The one on the outside, with her hair swept back, is gripping the arm of the other, at the elbow. She has on a tight blouse that is not tucked into her white skirt. She has a bracelet on her left wrist, same hand that is carrying a slender purse.

The other woman has on a white dress. To her right and in back of her is a Vietnamese man—white shirt, white shorts, white socks, dark loafers—standing near two parked bicycles with his arms folded, looking in the opposite direction of the women. There is a poster on a tree near him.

To the left and behind the outside woman is a young guy who looks like a military cadet, in a uniform and beret.

When I see these black-and-white photos, I can't help but wonder what happened to these people, how many are still alive, how many became victims of the American War.

I bought a thick envelope's worth of small photographs from a woman in a shop beyond the tourist areas of Saigon. She told me that she had an entire floor of stuff at her home on the outskirts of town. I went out there by motorbike one afternoon. She did indeed have an entire floor, filled with old stuff in wooden crates and cardboard boxes spread out across the floor. It was the top floor of her big house, and like many such top floors, it had a roof and a low wall that was maybe three feet high but was otherwise open. There were box after box of guns and ammunition and fully loaded magazines; military logbooks and journals, old electronic equipment that looked quaint, uniforms, helmets, bayonets; toys, books in Russian, French, English and Vietnamese. The guns were jammed from the humidity; some still had ammunition. It was all worth of a fortune, but, unfortunately, she wanted a fortune for it.

TAKE 53

SMALL DISPLAY AD FROM COAST REPORTER, A WEEKLY NEWSPAPER OUT OF SECHELT, BRITISH COLUMBIA, PROBABLY FROM 1998

I took this ad out, hoping to get some mosaic work. Several years earlier while plying my trade as a landscaper, I was asked to make a small deck using cement and various chunks of broken brick and pieces of tile laying about the property. This was at Jericho Beach in Vancouver. I'd never done anything like that, but the results were satisfying to the homeowner, and I was encouraged to pursue this kind of thing. Eventually, I did walls, walkways, signs and fireplace hearths. As well, I made mosaic floors, sinks and cabinets, and wall pieces for my own pleasure. I used stone, tile, glass, pebbles, shells—whatever I thought might work.

That ad, which ran in seven consecutive issues, got me absolutely no work; there was not even a single phone call. I made a mosaic design on a three-foot-long piece of plywood and affixed it to the side of my van, along with a phone number. There were no calls, no questions. Any work I got came via word of mouth.

I started including mosaic work in art shows that I was part of. At one gallery, I showed a birdhouse set on a column. I'd gotten a cardboard tube used in concrete work, filled it with cement around a thick piece of rebar and, after it had dried, mosaicked the outside and put a colourfully painted birdhouse of my own design on top. An elderly lady living in Sechelt bought the piece on the condition I install it in her yard, which I did.

After that I made other towers but in more elaborate form. One done in 2000 in Mexico still sits outside an apartment building in Puerto Escondido; another that looks like some weird pagan monument lives in the southern Ontario countryside. I still do this sort of thing; in fact, feel free to contact me about commissions!

TAKE 54

RECEIPT FOR ONE NIGHT'S STAY AT THE BURRARD MOTOR INN ON BURRARD STREET IN VANCOUVER, DATED NOVEMBER 10, 1985

Just looking at this receipt vividly recalls the mood I was in when I stayed there. I had just gotten back from a month in Fiji, moving around from island to island in the sunshine; in fact, I had a pass on Sunflower Air and could go wherever I wished. One day, walking along the shore of a remote island, I was hailed by a man and woman in a dugout canoe. They invited me to their own island, even more remote than the one I was on. When we arrived, I was directed to a vacant *bure* in which I lived for five days, and took part in the life of the thirty or forty people on the tiny island.

And here I was back in Vancouver on a typical November day (or April or June day, for that matter); it was dark and gloomy and the rain fell relentlessly.

TAKE 55

LETTER FROM CHARLES EMILE BEDAUX, BOX 7, PLACENTIA, CA

Charles Emile was the son of the infamous Charles Eugène Bedaux (1887–1943), rags-to-riches immigrant to America (from France) who devised a system to make work more efficient and was mistakenly called a "speed-up" king by organized labour (although AFL-CIO used his methods in their offices), accused of being a spy and Nazi collaborator, hosted the wedding of the Duke and Duchess of Windsor and then distanced himself from them. He tried to build a pipeline to carry peanut oil across Africa, a project shut down by the Nazis. He was arrested and held in North Africa, along with his son Charles Emile. I wrote the first—and to this day, the only—biography of this fascinating man, the father: *The Price of Power* (Doubleday, NY, 1984).

During the course of my research I made contact with Charles Emile, later I visited him in California, and after that we went to Europe, courtesy of a film crew, who followed me during my investigations. The result was a film called *Looking for Bedaux*.

Here is the letter, one of several. This one was written after the book came out:

Dear Jim,
    Am so mad. I could spit! Was so tickled to hear you in Palm Springs when you phoned. Jotted No. on scrap paper on our breakfast table. Mon, Tue. Wed. Carmen put mail at my place. Coming in between 8 & 8.30 each evening too bushed to do anything but eat & sleep. Come Thursday searched for that scrap of paper with your No. cause I'd have driven to Palm Springs, if you hadn't got a car or met you ½ way somewhere. Searched everywhere—(at least got a lot filed away)—not to be found. Kept hoping you'd phone again. No luck. When I get out from under this job within a month, will rush to finish MS, then maybe can come visit you.
    All the best for Holidays & your writings!
    Chuck

Charles Emile grew up estranged from his father and disliking him intensely. His mother remarried the owner of the *St. Louis Post-Dispatch*. Any meetings with his father were awkward at best. Finally, imprisoned together, first in Paris and then in Algeria, he came, at least, to understand him. He paid me the best compliment: "It was only after reading your book that I came to like my father."

And not until 2010 has there been any work published that affirms my view of Charles Eugène Bedaux, and that work is *Americans in Paris* by Charles Glass, former ABC news anchor and hostage of the Mujahedeen. As I wrote in my book, the French didn't give the Légion d'honneur to collaborators, nor do they name streets after them.

Charles Emile was a kind, curious, sensitive man. I enjoyed his letters and his company. He broke down in tears when I showed him letters written by his father to associates bragging about his son.

TAKE 56

BUSINESS CARD OF HERBERT GEORGE BIGELOW

There is a connection here to Take 55.

Herbert Bigelow and Charles Emile never met, but the former became, in 1964, the secretary to Charles Eugène's second wife, Fern. I made contact with Herbert Bigelow, a tall, elegant man who had throat cancer and spoke through a voice box inserted in his neck, hidden by a ubiquitous ascot. Herbert maintained an apartment in Paris in rue Saint-Honoré and a country place, La Ferme Rose, at Chalo-Saint-Mars. He'd worked for Fern, mainly at the Chateau de Candé near Tours, and watched her grow batty over the years. He told me that not long after he'd met Fern, she began to hoard such things as canned goods and toilet paper, Kleenex and rubber bands. He was a storehouse of information about Fern, Candé and Charles. He had all her and Charles's diaries that he spread out on tables for me at Chalo-Saint-Mars, but alas, I was only allowed a few hours with them.

I introduced Herbert and Canadian filmmaker George Ungar, who made the feature-length documentary, *The Champagne Safari*. This film took the line that Bedaux was a collaborator, despite all the evidence I provided George to the contrary. But that's another story. It is a good film.

TAKE 57

ENTRY RECEIPT FOR THE CHAPEL DESIGNED BY THE MULTI-TALENTED JEAN COCTEAU AT VILLEFRANCHE-SUR-MER

This is the Chapelle de Saint-Pierre des Pêcheurs. Entry fee was 2 euros in 2007. I had been there thirty-seven years earlier, and it looked so much different than I remembered but still impressive. Cocteau—poet, playwright, novelist, filmmaker, artist—is, I believe, a much underrated figure, particularly in regard to his art. It is his films that get all the attention now, although personally I find them too mannered and obvious. Critics have said the same things about his plays and novels. His reputation suffers posthumously for the same reason he gained success while he was living: his personality. He was considered by many to be a gadfly, responsible for facile work. Yet his artwork is playful and touching, and if his drawing is reminiscent of Picasso's, so what?

TAKE 58

PIECE OF FADED SPIRAL NOTEBOOK PAPER WITH THE HEADING, IN PENCIL, MY HANDWRITING, "SHANGHAI ALLEY, 1937"

In 1998, I published a crime novel called *Shanghai Alley*, set in 1937. The title is taken from the name of the first street in Vancouver where Chinese people settled. I didn't do much research because I wanted to imagine and invent my own Shanghai Alley, but I did look up an old city directory to get an idea of what was going on in the narrow little lane. On the piece of notebook paper, I wrote down the names of the five businesses on the street:

Geo Yim-barber
Koug Hing Co-hd goods
Kuoug Chen-barber
Sing Keu-dramatic society
Lee On Wo Co-groc

Not long after writing the book, but years before it was published, I worked as a sort of glorified extra on a TV episode, one scene of which was shot on Shanghai Alley, which by then consisted of vacant buildings surrounded by a chain-link fence. I tried to imagine the action in my book taking place in this sterile space, but that was impossible. It was no longer a site for drama.

TAKE 59

BUSINESS CARD OF ONE ROBERTA DENTON, SUPERVISOR OF BLANDFORD CEMETERY, 319 S. CRATER ROAD, PETERSBURG, VA. 23803; TELEPHONE: (804) 733-2397

Although I have spent many hours over many years wandering around Blandford Cemetery—which is adjacent to Petersburg Battlefield Park, a battlefield of the War Between the States (Civil War)—I haven't spent any of those hours recently. I suppose the card was sent to me by my late brother, David, who took photographs of the markers of my mother and father.

Although I grew up in Philadelphia, the mainly Italian area of South Philadelphia, I spent many of those childhood summers in Virginia, on a small farm near Petersburg. I often accompanied my Aunt Louise, who was divorced and lived with her parents in a settlement called Disputanta. Louise was always driving somewhere and leaving me off while she did whatever she did. One thing she did, I'm pretty sure, was conduct an affair with a man who owned another battlefield in Petersburg, Fort Sedgewick, called "Fort Hell." While she was inside with him, I'd wander around the place looking for mortar balls and, if I dug deep enough, I'd find arrow heads. She'd call for me when it was time to leave. Another place she left me was Blandford Cemetery. She'd drop me off, and I'd make for the oldest parts of the cemetery to read the gravestones. Some of the people buried there had been born in the early 1700s. I could easily spend two or three hours figuring out the consequences of their ages, wondering what life was like for some fellow who lived from 1752 to 1814. I'd wonder what he might have been doing during the War of Independence.

My grandfather died in 1954 and is buried at Blandford. I remember the day of the funeral. I was playing outside in the farmyard, and my mother got angry at me for not treating the occasion with the appropriate solemnity. Louise said, "Kathleen, he doesn't understand."

I can recall little about the funeral service, but the burial at Blandford is clear in my mind. The ceremony bored me, and I wandered off, but not before they lowered the casket into the ground. I was fascinated by the procedure, the thick ropes that looped under the coffin and were held by men on either side. I watched them play out the ropes, and the gaudy box disappeared. Not too far from where all that happened, I came upon a large carved angel. I read the dates on the tombstone: it was a little girl who had lived only nine months. Below the dates, the mason had chiseled the line, "God's Little Angle."

I stood there staring, wondering how could they not have realized the mistake. The girl's brief life had been contained in the year 1951. So three years had passed. Maybe her parents couldn't afford to replace the stone. Twenty years later, I returned to Blandford Cemetery, but the angel was gone, finally replaced. But just a couple of years ago, thinking about that poor little girl, I wrote a poem/song called "God's Little Angle" that was included on a CD of the same name.

My grandmother was buried at Blandford in 1985; she lived to be ninety-eight years old. My mother died in 1997 in New Jersey and my father in New Jersey in 2004; they were both cremated and their ashes interred at Blandford. It's difficult to think of any part of my Italian old man, a true street character born and raised among cement and redbrick, a real wise guy, resting there in the southern earth, a Yankee among all those rebels.

TAKE 60

STUDIO PHOTOGRAPH OF JOSEPH ISAAC "IKE" CLANTON, TAKEN AT TOMBSTONE, ARIZONA, 1880, THE YEAR BEFORE HE AND HIS BROTHER BILLY WERE GUNNED DOWN BY THE EARPS AND THEIR SYPHILITIC JUNKIE DENTIST PAL, DOC HALLIDAY (YES, HALLIDAY).

This photo relates to Take 59 in that my grandmother was Reatha Dolby. Her maiden name was Bailey but her mother's maiden name was Clanton. So those were my relatives, murdered at Tombstone. This was always part of family lore, but I never paid much attention to it until I was contacted by a western historian named Alford Taylor who had traced the genealogy of the Clantons.

The Clantons were outlaws, no doubt about that. The first time the word "cowboy" was used in the *Tombstone Epitaph* was to describe the gang of cattle rustlers that worked for and with Newman Clanton, the father of the clan that made forays over into Mexico to bring back cattle. The Earps were a difficult breed of outlaw; they hid behind the system. They were Republican Party hacks. Were they around in recent times, they'd have been henchmen for Bush and Cheney.

TAKE 61

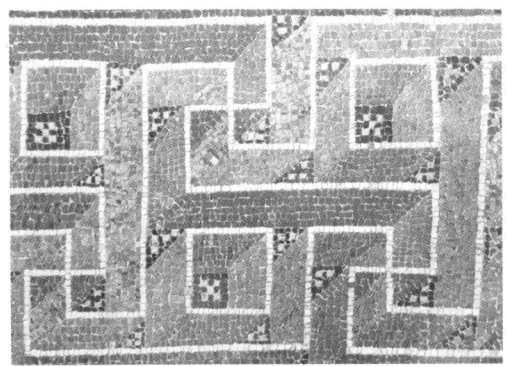

POSTCARD FROM RAVENNA, ITALY

Picture side shows a detail of the "Greek fret" from the Mausoleo Di Galla Placidia, a masterpiece of mosaic art.

TAKE 62

"HAPPY NEW YEAR," A 46¢ CANADIAN STAMP FEATURING A DRAWING OF GUY LOMBARDO, PROBABLY DONE BY SOMEONE WHO WAS NOT A FAN

It looks like a goofy Guy, a real square at the party, looking for a lampshade. Most jazzmen considered the music of this native son of London, Ontario, to be too corny to bear, but somebody liked it because few, if any, artists sold more records. There is a debate over whether he sold 200 million or 300 million. Guy Lombardo was also a fanatic about speedboat racing, and once held the world's water-speed record.

TAKE 63

LETTER WRITTEN TO ME ON A PAPER NAPKIN WITH BLACK FELT PEN BY MY BROTHER DAVE

"Dear Jim,
Stopped my new part-time Ice Cream Truck. At the famous South Philly's Melrose Diner (Broad & Passyunk) for a bite.
Hope you are fine.
Here is your Passport paper. I read the back and was wondering if you would be able to apply?
Take it easy!
L. Dave"

I'm trying to remember what this was about. I believe it refers to a form for passport renewal that had been mailed to me by the U.S. government. But I had already moved to Canada and renounced my U.S. citizenship; therefore, the note must date to 1969, as that is the year my one and only U.S. passport would have expired. A couple of years later, my brother moved to Canada, married a Montreal woman and stayed in this country for fifteen years before returning to the Philadelphia area. Eight years my junior, he died while I was preparing this book.

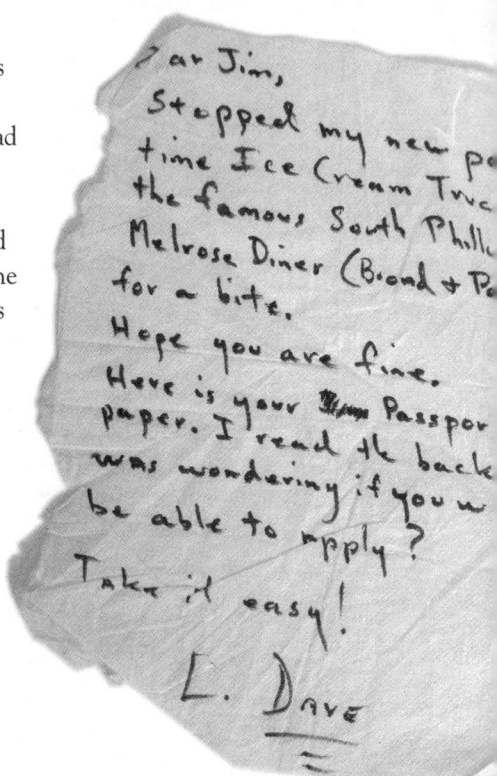

TAKE 64

COLLAGE ON A PIECE OF CHARRED WOOD, DONE BY ME IN PUERTO ESCONDIDO, OAXACA, MEXICO, 2007

I travelled to Puerto Escondido, spending various amounts of time there, between 1991 and 2007. In the winter of 1999–2000, my friends Paul Murphy and Bradley Benson and I rented a large, ground-floor apartment with a courtyard. Those were good times that featured sunshine and interesting people, Mexican and not.

I should not have messed with that good memory by going back to Puerto Escondido seven years later but, alas… The town has gotten expensive and is, consequently, overrun by tourists to the point where certain areas might be in many another tropical tourist town in Mexico, Hawaii, Costa Rica or Goa, wherever there are dark-skinned people waiting on white ones.

Nevertheless, my friend and I got a cheap apartment and stayed for a month. The landlady kept ferrets, minks and hamsters in cages.

I had no art supplies but bought some glue and stuck a matchbook cover (classicos), a broken lighter, a leaf, a mass card, scraps from newspapers, four slivers of wood, a sketch of a skull and a leaf, to a piece of plywood.

TAKE 65

PHOTOGRAPH OF WAVERY MOSAIC TOWER

The owner of the apartment building where I stayed with my friends in Escondido in 1999–2000, as mentioned above, commissioned me to make the sculpture in the photograph.

When you ask directions in Mexico, whether you are directed to go straight, left or right, the person you ask will invariably make the same gesture with his hand and arm. It's a sort of casual double or triple waving of the hand, the hand going left, right and straight ahead. They don't want to disappoint by telling you they don't know, so this way all possibilities are covered. I, therefore, called this piece *Mexican Directions*. A cord ran up through the tower and light shone through the wine-bottle bottoms.

It was still in place in 2007, but the bottles and the light bulb had been broken.

TAKE 66

BUSINESS CARD FOR ONE HILLIARD LYLE, "HOTEL CONSULTANT"

I went and saw this man in Vancouver as a favour to someone with an interest in mercenary soldiers, soldiers of fortune and certain types of criminals. Lyle lived in a small West End apartment and had been the manager of the lounge at the Sylvia Hotel when it was the only establishment in town that sold alcoholic beverages to a mixed clientele. He was also the man who, in 1959, brokered the deal between Errol Flynn and the doctor who bought his yacht.

Lyle was one of the five people, including the star's sixteen-year-old girlfriend, in the apartment that afternoon when Flynn announced he was feeling tired and was going to lie down for a while. "I shall return," Flynn said, as he went into the bedroom. He didn't. He lay down forever.

For decades the rumour went around that a distraught Beverley Aadland, having requested some time alone at the morgue with Flynn's body, cut off his penis for a souvenir and was later apprehended by the coroner on the Cambie Street Bridge with said organ in her handbag. I was one of many who believed this story, though I pride myself on knowing the real story behind these Hollywood tales—like the one about Jayne Mansfield's head being severed in her fatal car crash. (She suffered a slight cut on her neck.) As for Flynn's death and his member, the Vancouver coroner Glen McDonald eventually wrote the story. It was discovered that the actor's good-sized organ had large warts on its head. McDonald and his assistant had never seen warts of that size; at least, not in that place. The assistant wished to remove the warts to display during a talk he was to deliver soon. McDonald refused him permission, but when the coroner left the autopsy room, the assistant cut them off anyway. McDonald discovered the warts in a jar of formaldehyde and scotch-taped them back on. The corpse was sent on its way to its burial place in Hollywood.

HILLIARD LYLE
HOTEL CONSULTANT

1002 - 1655 HARO STREET
VANCOUVER, B.C. V6G 1G9   682-7607

As for Hilliard Lyle Jr., he was not a mercenary, soldier of fortune and criminal like his father had been. After years spent fighting for right-wing regimes or in right-wing revolutions, Lyle Sr. was called in to put down the Winnipeg General Strike of 1919.

In the late '20s, while living in northern Alberta, Lyle Sr.

murdered his wife and his daughter. Not being able to find his son and anxious to be done with it, he killed himself.

"I hid behind the outhouse," Hilliard Lyle Jr. told me.

The doctor who administered Demerol to Errol Flynn to stimulate his heart in that West End apartment in 1959 was Glen Gould's uncle, Grant A. Gould.

TAKE 67

A PICTURE POSTCARD OF THREE EMUS

Move your head or move the card, and the focus shifts. There's a kind of 3-D effect. On the back, written in one corner, is my name and Vancouver address and the date 1982. In another corner is the last name and first initial of the sender, and an address in Padston, Sydney, Australia.

I have no idea who this person is. I am, however, fond of emus, and was in 1982. Perhaps this is from someone I talked with about emus; it occurs to me that the sender might be a large woman. Female emus, as many know, are always larger than their male mates.

TAKE 68

8½" X 11" INCH SHEET OF PHOTOCOPY PAPER WITH THREE COLOUR PICTURES: ONE TAKEN ON THE OUTSKIRTS OF PHNOM PENH, CAMBODIA; TWO TAKEN IN HO CHI MINH CITY (SAIGON), VIETNAM

In one of the Vietnam photos, a shy young woman is holding a red hammock in the web between the thumb and first finger of her left hand; she's smiling but not looking at the camera. In back of her are shelves with other hammocks in clear plastic bags. The other Saigon photo is of a young guy in a green "GUESS" T-shirt holding a blue hammock in front of him with both hands. He is also smiling. He's not looking at the camera but isn't as shy as the young woman.

In the third picture, a beautiful little girl, perhaps ten years old, is sitting on a tall pile of hammocks and looking directly at the camera; her mother is to her left, bending over to look for something in the pile, her back to the camera. Beyond them are other children, and at the open door, a young guy in black slacks and white T-shirt is looking down the street, his head in profile.

I decided I was going to make a lot of money, bringing hammocks to Canada to sell. I wasn't going to buy hammocks from Mexican sweatshops but from people who made them by hand or on handmade machines. Southeast Asia seemed perfect for this, and I went and found the right people. The Vietnamese kids were working in a very small shop at an ancient wooden machine that resembled a loom. I was taken there by an old friend named Hu, a Saigon go-to guy.

In Phnom Penh, I heard stories about a woman who made hammocks by hand and set out to find her. I spent an interesting four hours driving around the outer reaches of the city on a motorbike with a guy named Nuoug before locating her. She is the lady with her back to the camera. She pushed a cart around to textile factories, loading it with cast-off scraps of cloth. She'd cut the cloth into small strips and tie them together until she had a complete hammock. She was so grateful when I bought fifty of them that I was embarrassed.

I heard about other people in the two countries who made hammocks out of the bark of a certain kind of tree, from lianas, from old army uniforms. Those I would search out on the next trip; these I would take back and sell through small shops in Canada. The hammocks would go for much less than the shoddy merchandise sold at the usual Yuppie outdoor outlets, and the buyer would know they'd be helping poor people in the slums of Southeast Asia. I would leave behind-the-scenes photographs at every outlet that took the hammocks. Who could resist a hammock handmade by the hardworking mother of the heartbreakingly beautiful little girl in the photograph?

Most everyone could, it turned out, and did. I don't think I sold more than five hammocks through stores. I sold some by word of mouth. I still have plenty of them left. If you're interested, write to me care of the publisher!

TAKE 69

JOTTINGS ON 3" X 6" LINED PAPER TORN FROM A SPIRAL POCKET NOTEBOOK, EARLY '70S

Vancouver, Denman Plaza: old blue-haired English ladies sipping tea and discussing their diets, veiny hands fluttering on canes. Beach bums with bleached eyebrows surveying the boys. Would-be gigolos from Yugoslavia posing, soft stomachs pushing out from flowered body shirts. Sienna tiles and soft neons. Dozens of beautiful women in high heel shoes. Shoppers and tanned tennis players. It's a long way from E. Hastings where right now, Saturday morning, Mr. Jones and the hookers, the pimps with holes in their socks, no Cadillacs at the door, the winos in the freight yards, pensioners in Cambie rooms, Chinese octogenarians are just waking up, Saturday, hot and cold flashes, tubercular coughs, phlegm-y hacking coughs, sore ___(?), dehydrated, discovering fresh abrasions, turning on Saturday cartoons on TV in the darkened rooms, pissing in the bottle kept under the bed, moaning. How much better to be a Denman Street faggot than a forty-year-old queer at Hastings and Main, peddling your ass at Hastings and Main... A few days ago, I took a crippled old lady's dying husband up to a penthouse apartment on the Bay (English Bay). The polished coffee table ladened with brand new novels.

TAKE 70

OLD-STYLE MAN'S WALLET THAT WAS KEPT IN THE INSIDE BREAST POCKET OF A SUIT JACKET OR SPORTS COAT. MADE OF ENGLISH MOROCCO LEATHER. IT OPENS TO REVEAL POCKETS, STAMPED, GOLD ON BLACK: "BAGGAGE CHECKS, LANDING CARD, TICKETS, PASSPORT, FOREIGN MONEY."

In LANDING CARD, is a business card from the VRISA Bookshop in Quetzaltenango, Guatemala. A great and unexpected find in that interesting town in the highlands. I've been there twice but not for ten years. The shop offers, or offered, "New & Used Books in English," as well as maps and coffee. They would even rent you a bike. It was across from the post office.

The card has the names of the owners written in ballpoint pen: Colin Shade and Julia Shade. In parentheses is "Andrea Berry."

In "TICKETS" is a receipt from the Stein Inn in Mason City, Iowa, dated August 2, 1984.

Mason City is near Britt, which every year since 1904 has hosted the Hobo Convention. I first attended as a hobo—or so I fancied myself, riding freight trains around America—in 1964; I went back in 1965. The town used to make a big deal of the convention, offering relatively big-name entertainment and parades. One of those years, they had the Ink Spots performing. By the '70s and '80s it was not as grand. I went three or four times, either as a journalist or just an observer. In 1984, I visited the hospital in Mason City to pay a call on the Pennsylvania Kid, a real old-time 'bo who had known Floyd Wallace (called the Greeley Kid), who had been my friend and mentor on the ways of the road and of roughing it, and of generally living as free as possible in an increasingly homogenized world.

The Pennsylvania Kid was dying. He was astounded to have a visitor. We talked until his voice grew weak and weary. Later I stopped in Mason City to have a beer and think about the passing scene.

Also, in the same pocket is a small sketch or cartoon cut from a magazine in New Zealand. It's of a rugby player called J. Bissett from the South Melbourne Club in Australia. His head is in profile. I clipped this sketch because the guy looks exactly like Neal Cassady.

In BAGGAGE CHECKS, there is a small coloured picture of the Virgen de Guadalupe, patron of Latin America and the Philippines, and a clipping from a newspaper with the headline "Gypsy beatified—a first for the church." I don't know the date of the clipping or in which paper the story appeared. On the reverse side is the bottom part of an ad for a jeweler. The name of the business is obscured, but there is a Church Street address in Toronto. It's probably from the *Star*, pre-makeover.

The article has the subhead, "Pope John Paul honors martyr of Spanish Civil War." I must have clipped this not only because I have obscure hagiographic interests, but also because I sensed the anti-Republican sentiment that was to be revealed between the lines—the historical anti-Republican stance of the Catholic Church. "Several thousand Gypsies from all over Europe joined the crowd in St. Peter's Square to attend a mass in honor of Ceferino Jimenez Malla and four other people beatified by the Pope. Beatification is the last formal step before possible sainthood."

The story relates that Malla was killed by Republican forces during the Spanish Civil War after being arrested for defending a priest. He was killed when he refused to renounce his faith.

Also beatified was Florentino Asensio Barroso, bishop of Barbastro in Spain. He was also killed by Republican forces.

Two Italians were beatified that day, one from the north of Italy, one from the south, as well as a Guatemalan nun.

The article ends with the note that since becoming Pope in 1978, John Paul "has beatified 768 people and canonized 276, more than all of this century's other popes put together."

I know that among this number were plenty of Africans. Makes for good politics.

In FOREIGN CURRENCY is a photograph of me taken on the island of Taveuni, one of the Fijis. Dressed in white pants and shoes, wearing a light grey T-shirt, hair parted in the middle, I am standing before the sign marking the international dateline. It is on two palm-tree posts with arrows pointing to TODAY and YESTERDAY.

And lo and behold, just now as I'm putting this photograph back in its pocket, I discover a Swiss fifty-franc bill with a photo of Sophie Taueber-Arp, 1889–1943.

Born Sophie Taueber in Switzerland, she was a painter and designer and one of the original Dadaists. I like to think she might have appreciated this book about my Sweet Assorted box. She added the Arp to her name when she married Jean in 1922.

TAKE 71

INVOICE FROM TORONTO LIFE PUBLISHING COMPANY INDICATING THAT THEY PAID ME EIGHT HUNDRED DOLLARS ($800) FOR AN ESSAY ON "ADVENTURE"

I remember that I enjoyed writing this piece and taking a few jabs at those who debase the word and concept of "adventure." I don't have and never have had a copy of the printed version of this essay, which I believe appeared in one of the "Men's" supplements to *Toronto Life*. I did two other ones, on cigars and women's lingerie. Never seen those either.

Anyway, I maintained, and still maintain, that adventure is primarily an attitude. Not long before I wrote this essay, a man

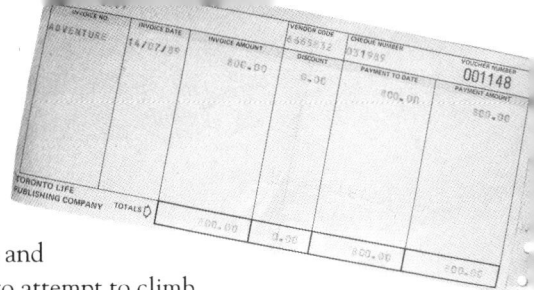

telephoned and introduced himself as an "adventurer." He proudly announced that he and a couple of friends were going to attempt to climb Mount Everest and he hoped I would endeavour to write a story about him. He was a business guy, and so were his friends. He said they were all "goal oriented."

I believe I wrote in my article that the qualities needed to climb Everest are not all that different than those required of a good corporate manager. Whereas someone with an adventuresome spirit, like my late, great friends Marcel Horne and Floyd Wallace, the latter mentioned in Take 70, were adventurers all day and all night. I'd rather hear Marcel's account of his bus ride from Toronto to Leamington than anyone else's report on his or her Everest expedition.

The would-be mountain climber spoke about all the suspected hardships. Not to belittle him or his hardships, but they're nothing compared to what a single mother with one or more children and no job faces every morning of her life. I wrote that, too.

TAKE 72

FOUR-AND-A-HALF PAGES OF TYPED-UPON (BY ME) BRITTLE YELLOW FOOLSCAP, HELD TOGETHER WITH A RUSTY PAPERCLIP

I'm roaming, free associating. At first, I was vaguely uncomfortable re-reading this after thirty-five-plus years; it's maybe sentimental, callow and corny or overly romantic, but what the hell. It expresses how I felt and often still feel. I think I called it "Visions in the Glossy Ice," the idea being that I was staring at the ice cubes in my twelfth vodka in the wee hours, having these thoughts.

The half page begins in the middle of a line...

"...now. I know where my responsibilities lie. I am waking up and going out into those red brick streets and cutting to the theatre to see Randolph Scott, I am holding my tenor and caressing the bell, I will blow hours of Saturday afternoon blues for no reason than I want to blow. I will not be a sullen spoiled electric guitarist of suburban rock music throwing up on stage because I can't drink, because I hate the world and therefore have to make this pathetic gesture. I will not have nine million dollars worth of electronics to bring out my sound. I will wail with my piano player who'll have no circuits to interfere with his body action. The bassist will be bent, and bent over his huge scarred anachronism, gooping with long bony fingers, laying down a line that is eternal. The skinny little trumpet player will sing so pure everybody'll be amazed. I will step to the fore and strut my noise like Gene Ammons or be as lyrically wise as Al Cohn. I won't come home til late Saturday night, I'll get through awful Sunday which turns fine at 7:30 PM when I hatch my secret plan to skip school the next day to hide in...where to hide in South Philadelphia? I'll go downtown and shine shoes or skip school in Toronto where nobody cares about a nine-year-old kid in the streets filled with immigrants. I'll go to the movies on Yonge Street or play in High Park, later that night I'll sneak into the Dollar upstairs, crawl under a table and look up ladies' dresses, or at forbidden milk white strippers' breasts...I will not play if I don't feel like it. I will quit and go race sports cars like Allen Eager. I will grow my hair long and red like Chet Baker and slur and miss notes because I have been in jail too long to care. I'll call myself Kai Winding and everyone'll mispronounce my name. I'll get a crew-cut and Hawaiian shirts and I can be anybody in cool jazz. Drugstores will be robbed because I was Stan Getz. I'll never be Buddy Rich because he makes me sick. Instead I'll become the black Clark Gable (Dexter Gordon) and call my girls from mysterious telephone booths and in my spare time give lessons to young John Coltrane. Or maybe just vanish into obscurity, be an eccentric music teacher like Lennie Tristano, go to Europe a la Brew Moore, seek anonymity in the bottle like Gene

Quill. I'll long for the old days
of the Our Gang comedies
when my father could leave
me (Saturday afternoon) in the
playground while he hung around
the Italian social club talking with
the judges and ward heelers. These
were the days, the very last of them
too, when fathers played ball after work
and little kids watched with mustard on
their mouths, when men didn't have to be
ashamed to have great buddies who were also
men, when you could hang around the corner
without being arrested, when you could fix the
tractor with baling wire and a pair of pliers, before
there was an expressway through the swimming
hole and you didn't see IBM, Honeywell and Litton
Industries on your Sunday drives. Yes, by God, those
were the days when women stayed pregnant in the
kitchen, and your government was lying to you but at
least you didn't know it. When you had John Foster Dulles
instead of Henry Kissinger. When girls didn't go down on
you on the first date. Yes, if we could only keep funky and get
back. I mean if there were *Penthouse* photo essays, an actual
living Charlie Parker, garter belts and '49 Mercurys, no CIA
assassins—hold it, I hedged back there, there must be something
other than *Penthouse* photo essays which I don't look at that often
anyway. And maybe girls weren't any different either. But, I do
want to be modern. I demand, however, that there be something
other than Johnny Carson and McDonalds and five-and-a-half-hour
flights to Paris. Perhaps it's not so much that my soul is haunted by
nostalgia but that I yearn for a new tomorrow. I want Jackie Coogan
[Cooper] to wake up Wallace Beery who's sleeping with Marie
Dressler and then I want us all to fly to Mars with Errol Flynn as

our pilot. Where is the new Charlie Parker to supply the in-flight music? Tell me and I shall cast aside childish things; I will no longer weep for Jean Harlow and fenders of old Plymouths. I refuse to walk around the earth for Guru Maharaji. Gene Ammons, John Coltrane, Lester Young, Brew Moore, Lennie Tristano, George Wallington, Joe Albany all passed by. Where is the hipster so gone he falls out in the gutter and somebody cops his horn? His porkpie hat gone with the wind. Taxis splattering muddy rainwater on his zoot suit. The sports page of the *New York World* comes whipping down the street and covers his face. Bosox Edge Yanks, 2–1 on Zarilla 9th Inning Homer…splattering muddy rainwater on his zoot suit?

Zoot. Zoot Sims.

How did he get that name? He is now wearing an inexpensive off-the-rack insurance man's suit with a skinny tie and faded orange shirt—there's the clue, that trace of, when? 1947, Woody Herman's band, The Four Brothers, their horns, young heavyset Zoot with curly blond hair brushed back, large head bowed to his tenor. Just a couple years earlier at nineteen he'd cut his first record, sounding like Ben Webster. He wore a broad-shoulder striped suit with baggy pegged-at-the-ankles pants. Dizzy Gillespie would blush…over the years he has gotten sort of laid-back looking, slow, lumbering almost, except when he plays, same power and drive that cut Sonny Stitt one evening, 1961, at the Half Note. The drummer and bass player tonight are modern cats with long, styled hair and moustaches, flowered shirts. But the piano player is a skeletal throwback to 1949. He looks like every gaunt junkie hipster of that long-gone era. He's hunched over the keys with eyes closed muttering phrases to himself and…the audacity of it…actually stealing the show. A marvellous display of nerve, he is hogging solos, causing Zoot to keep licking the mouthpiece in false starts. That right hand seems to have a life of its own, travelling up and down the keys like some kind of frenetic animal or crazy wind-up toy. Even some of the diners look up over their forks. Zoot's expression has changed by the third set to bemused resignation. He must be thinking of decades past when he and everybody was like this kid, when this same music was the end all and be all, the only answer to anything. How could he get angry? He steps forward and his horn gleams in the light, he bends back at the waist and swings with "All the Things You Are," providing a challenge to his young piano player who realizes and attacks the keyboard with shiny eyes and determined clenched jaw. It's the best number of the evening and when it's over Zoot gulps down the last of his drink and ever so slightly nods at the kid. End of set. They walk off, twenty-five years separating them. The piano player can't conceal a smile of accomplishment. He is wearing a colourful sport shirt with rolled short sleeves and he takes a seat with two girls but he just stares at his glass. He is somewhere else, he is with the First Herd getting off a bus in Chicago. Outside is not snowy Queen Street and glass towers but a warm spring evening on 52nd St. with the neon cocktail glasses glowing with promise, and legends passing through historic doorways. He exists outside his rightful place in time and he knows it, he will not touch his glass and disturb the visions in the glossy ice."

TAKE 73

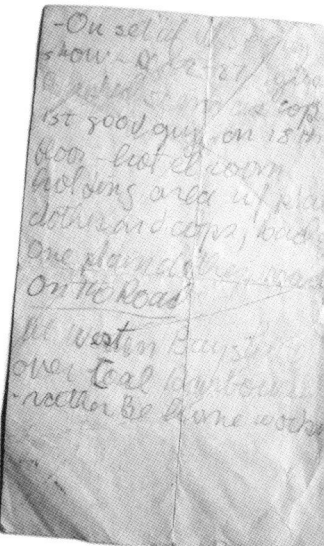

NOTE ON PIECE OF PAPER TORN FROM NOTEPAD FROM A ROOM AT HOTEL IN VANCOUVER

"On set of *Wiseguy* TV show—Dec. 2/87—just finished scene as plainclothes cop, 1st ever 'good guy'—on 18th floor hotel room holding area w/plainclothes and cops, bad guy. One plainclothes reading *On the Road*.

At Westin Bayshore, over Coal Harbour—rather be home working."

TAKE 74

35 MM NIGHTTIME PHOTOGRAPH TAKEN AT TOK, ALASKA, BY ME, SOMETIME IN THE '90S

Photo shows a vertical, dimly lit motel sign, adjacent to which are two horizontal signs, the top, reading "TOK Liquor Mini Mart" and below that "TOK ALASKA WELCOMES YOU."

This photo is probably from my 1993 trip for *Equinox* magazine. But then again, I was in the Yukon and Alaska a couple of years earlier, trying to get a job. I believe the idea then was to make an effort to Pull Myself Up By The Bootstraps and be responsible, an idea that has never worked for me.

TAKE 75

PHOTOCOPY OF CLIPPING FROM THE PORT ARTHUR NEWS-CHRONICLE, DATED "SAT AUG 6, 1966," ADVERTISING THE APPEARANCE OF THE GREAT SINGER AND GUITARIST LONNIE JOHNSON IN THE MARINE ROOM AT THE SHORELINE MOTOR HOTEL, 61 CUMBERLAND STREET, PORT ARTHUR, ONTARIO

There is a picture of Lonnie that doesn't resemble Lonnie at all, but maybe it's just an old copy of a wrinkly old photograph. Underneath the picture, we read, "Johnson, a jazz-blues guitarist, has been around for decades, and has influenced more jazz guitar players than you can count. He has a brilliant original style that will dazzle you when he plays some amazing breaks with all the agility of a man a third his age. He is also an impressive singer of blues and pop ballads and his repertoire is so vast that he will never run out of songs!"

All that is true.

Lonnie Johnson came up to Toronto in 1965 for a gig and wound up basing himself in the city until he died in 1970. He loved the town, only venturing away from it to record in New York or when he had a gig such as this one or another in Ottawa. The response to his presence in Ottawa was so bad, however, that he was left seriously depressed for weeks. Very few people showed up, and the ones who did were not enamoured of what they heard. I'm reminded of Big Miller telling me that when he moved to Canada in the late '50s, audiences all expected him to do Louis Armstrong imitations, Pops evidently being the only black jazz image their minds could retain. Yet with Johnson, people were getting the personification of the history of the blues in all its ramifications. He could do anything and is considered by many to be the greatest guitar player in the history of the blues and the most versatile singer. He is my favourite, anyway, because he conveys the quality of sincerity no matter what kind of song he is singing, no matter what style.

The reaction to his appearance in Port Arthur was much more enthusiastic than it had been in Ottawa. He played to a packed house every night. By chance, my friend Nicky Drumbolis, raised in Port Arthur, was at the Marine Room a couple of nights during Lonnie's stay and, too young to get served, caught set after set from a doorway that gave onto an alley—the door being open in the August heat. Nicky says he was entranced by the greatness of what he heard.

Johnson died of injuries suffered in a traffic accident in Toronto. One story has it that he was hit by a streetcar; another, that a drunk driver hopped the curb and hit him as he walked along the sidewalk. Neither is true. Twenty-five-year-old David Hoskins was driving along Avenue Road, near Webster Street, when his car was rear-ended by another car, jumped the curb and ran Lonnie Johnson down. He was in the hospital for months and died a year later.

TAKE 76

FLYER, BLUE INK ON CHEAP PAPER, ADVERTISING THE CLOSED-CIRCUIT BROADCAST OF A BOXING MATCH AT NUMBER 1028 ARMENTA Y LOPEZ IN OAXACA, OAX

The fight was on January 16, 1999, between Mike Tyson and Francois Botha of South Africa. The show also featured two fights with Mexican competitors. Cover charge was 30 pesos. There is a cartoon drawing of Mike Tyson, teeth bared, looking very much like a mountain gorilla.

I went to the fight, which was projected on the wall of a garage, there being no screen, with my friend Paul Murphy. The garage was crowded. We were the only gringos. Nobody hassled us. Tyson was on a comeback and knocked Botha out.

TAKE 77

PAGE TORN FROM POCKET-SIZED SPIRAL NOTEBOOK; MY WRITING IN BLACK BALLPOINT PEN, FROM THE '70S

"At Poretta's Pizza, Robert & Harbord (Toronto), I come in and sit down in front of two guys philosophizing. 'You can't know the world. Only ideas are real.'

"Hmm, what would René Crevel think of that? Near me, oblivious to this discussion, with brow wrinkled over a Harlequin romance, half in sun, half in shadow sits an attractive 30-year-old woman, chain smoking and coke drinking as she reads, absorbed in romance, dreaming of young lawyers and gridiron heroes, her pizza going cold. Mr Poretta, who looks like my father, waves his rolling pin in the air and mutters oaths about his son, who roars around the corner and jerks to a stop in the Morris-Mini delivery car. The philosophers depart and are replaced by a husky man in his late fifties who launches immediately into his adventures at the hospital. He grabs a 7-Up, orders a hamburger and complains about how he has to watch his diet. Curses the Doctors Hospital, complains about the $47 he paid for x-rays. Describes his slipped…"

Alas, it ends there in the middle of a sentence.

TAKE 78

SHEET OF NEWSPRINT PAPER

I was trying to write a haiku this particular day, October 17, 1988, while listening to CBC radio. I called it "Don't Be Cruel, A Morningside Haiku."

> Peter Gzowski
> Alive at Eleven
> Laughing at dead
> Elvis

TAKE 79

POSTCARD WITH COLOUR PHOTO OF LA GROTTE MIRACULEUSE, LOURDES, FRANCE

There aren't many people on the benches before the statue of Our Lady of Lourdes, which is in a niche in the rocks behind a fence. One person is sitting alone on the right in the back, the foreground of the photo; a couple on the left. Up front, in the background, is a figure in a wheelchair.

The card is postmarked 20 -10 1949, Tarbes, Hautes Pyrenees, and franked at 16 10. It is addressed to E.P. Bullenwell, Box 490, Yarmouth, Nova Scotia, Canada. Message reads, "All fine here. Mom—Pop—Cassie." There is not so much a signature as a swirl in green ink, like the message and address, underneath which are three gold dots.

I don't know where I picked up this postcard. I do have plenty of saints' cards. I am not a follower of any organized religion and find the Catholic Church abhorrent. Years ago, CBC show-host Michael

Enright got in trouble for stating on air that next to the mafia, the Catholic Church was the world's largest criminal organization. He was widely criticized for this, and I wrote a letter to the CBC, declaring that his only mistake was to put the Catholic Church in second place.

Yet, I am fascinated by the stories of many of the saints, people like Martin de Porres, Joseph of Cupertino, John of the Cross, Teresa of Avila and Saint Roch. Their stories put to shame the feeble inventions of the surrealists.

Less than an hour ago, and less than two blocks from where I sit now, reviewing these notes on Boulevard Barbes in Paris, October 2010, I saw in a shop on rue Labat a large calendar photo of Our Lady of Lourdes. The shop is owned by Hindus. I remember Jennifer Jones in the movie. She won the Academy Award.

TAKE 80

ELEVEN-COLUMN ITEM CLIPPED FROM THE VANCOUVER SUN AND HEADED "SKID ROADER LIVES IT UP." THE FIRST PARAGRAPH: "VANCOUVER POLICE ARE STILL TRYING TO FIND A SKID ROAD MAN WHO CASHED IN AN $11,000 WINDFALL THAT MISTAKENLY MADE ITS WAY ON TO HIS BANK RECORD."

It seems that a Vancouver doctor who was a steady customer at the Bank of Commerce was given a new number when he switched branches. Perhaps he was unaware of the new number or perhaps it was through force of habit that he kept using the old number to make deposits. The "Skid Road man" was forty-five years old but is not given a name in the newspaper story. Having been assigned the doctor's old number, he played it cool, letting the deposits add up before beginning to make a series of withdrawals. When he couldn't stand it any more, he purchased a certified cheque for $3,000, which he used to pay for a 1976 Cadillac. Then he withdrew $11,000 and took off. "Police believe the man is headed for Edmonton."

The story mentions that the bank paid the doctor his missing money, so here's hoping the forty-five-year-old resident of a "Powell Street hotel room" escaped the clutches of the law, or at least had a good time before he was caught.

TAKE 81

MANILA ENVELOPE FROM THE PROVINCE OF BRITISH COLUMBIA, MINISTRY OF HEALTH, DIVISION OF VITAL STATISTICS, ADDRESSED TO ME AT A BOX IN THE BENTALL STATION POST OFFICE IN VANCOUVER, AND POSTMARKED 13 VIII, 1987

Inside the envelope is a certificate of death for one ROSS AYNSLEY BROOKS and a receipt for $5. Ross died on December 1, 1946, at the age of sixty-three.

Several months earlier, I had gone to an exhibit at the Museum of Anthropology at the University of British Columbia (UBC) in Vancouver. On display were items from the backrooms of the museum, and I was attracted to a stone head that had been collected by one Ross Aynsley Brooks and donated to the museum by his wife. A card indicated that the origin of the sculpted head was not known, but there were more pieces in the workshops.

The more I thought about this curious head, the more interested I became in the story behind it. I, therefore, presented myself at the museum offices several days later, declaring that I wished to see more of the items from the Brooks donation. I assured the woman in charge that I was a serious investigator, had published books, and, when she doubted me, pointed to the Canadian *Who's Who* near her left elbow and said she could look me up.

I felt bad for doing that, but she was very rude. She told me that I was not a professor and didn't even have a PhD, which I already knew. The long and short of it was that I offered as a reference George Woodcock, who was on the museum board and didn't have a PhD either. She sighed exasperatedly but called Woodcock, who told her to let me in for god's sake. She allowed me to enter the backrooms but made it seem as if she was doing me a great favour.

I mention this because, quite frankly, I'm not big enough not to mention it; yet it also serves to indicate what many a serious independent researcher is up against. Ordinary professors are bad enough that one shouldn't also have to deal with their gatekeepers.

Mr. Brooks owned a business on Robson Street called Ye Old Curiosity Shop and was interested in all sorts of things; antiquities and British Columbia history, especially. On holidays and whenever he could steal a day or two, he enjoyed wandering around the province searching for old, interesting things, or else fishing on the Fraser River, in the vicinity of Hope. He spent thirty years at this and knew hundreds of people in the bush; he was especially fond of the local native people and spent many days and nights in their homes. On one fishing trip, a native man mentioned he had something to show Ross that he was sure Ross would be interested in. The man took him to a cave on the banks of the river. What Ross looked at were forty-some carved stone pieces, ranging in size from a foot to eight feet high. Ross Brooks told the native man that it was quite an accomplishment for his people to have carved so many sculptures so well. The native man shook his head. "It's not my people who did them. We just found them last week. Look closely: those faces are nothing like ours. Also the stone is not from around here."

The native man told Ross Brooks that he was free to do what he pleased with the statues. Brooks hired a truck and shipped them to Vancouver, where he began to study each piece individually. He pored over art and archaeology books and determined that the heads most closely resembled Oceanic and African carvings. He eventually contacted UBC and was, as his private journal indicated, patronized and treated shabbily. The professors insisted the carvings were done by Canadian native peoples.

Brooks was so upset and depressed by his treatment at the university that he went home and added a codicil to his will, indicating that the carvings were to go to his wife, but that upon her death, under no circumstances was the University of British Columbia to be given the pieces.

Eventually, Brooks decided that the stones were carved by Lemurians after the sinking of the continent of Atlantis, which was in the Pacific Ocean, or so he believed.

Anyway, Brooks died in 1946, and when his wife died in 1950, the stones were bequeathed to the dreaded university. In 1951, the university brought in outside experts to undertake a study of the stones that Brooks had found. The study concluded that the stones were *not* local; that they were hundreds of years old, and that dirt found on the pieces was similar in chemical composition to dirt found in Africa and the South Pacific.

None of this research was made public.

There is an entire history of British Columbia, of Canada, of North America, of the world, in fact, that is unspoken, hidden, obscured and downright denied. (George Woodcock, in fact, told me that he believed without reservation that the Plains Indians of North America were at one end of a great trade route, with the Ainu off the coast of Japan at the other.)

Why is this so? It can only be that the guardians of our past have reputations to protect, which is why David Thompson, in 1811, was the first non-native to penetrate to the Interior of B.C. and why Christopher Columbus discovered America.

TAKE 82

BUSINESS CARD FOR LA MANO MÁGICA, "GALLERIA DE ARTE CONTEMPORANEO Y POPULAR" IN OAXACA, OAXACA, ON M. ALCALÁ 203

I came upon La Mano Mágica in 1991 while living in an apartment above Bambi Bakery a few blocks away. The gallery was run by a gringa—a Canadian, if I remember correctly—married to a Mexican man who was a skillful weaver. I stayed in that apartment for three months after travelling around Mexico for a month. During that travelling time, I had made a little figure out of wood and odds and ends. I took it to the gallery and showed it to the woman, who surprised me by saying that if I had more pieces, she would represent me.

   In a place like Oaxaca, even then when it was not so overrun by tourists, it is not so easy to find interesting junk, because no one throws anything out that could conceivably be of use. But the Spanish lady who operated the Bambi and owned the building allowed me up onto the roof to explore. It took up a quarter of a block and was the scene of the Patrona's chicken-plucking operations. She had two machines that looked as if they were leftovers from the Inquisition. These were used to pluck the chickens. You fastened the bird—dead—in a holder in the middle of the machine, and it spun one way while the beaters attached to plates on either side of the bird spun the other. In a minute, you had a bald bird. Then into the boiling pot it went.

There was also a goodly amount of tubing from the plucking machines, as well as nuts and bolts, wires, cloth, wood scraps, metal screens, etc. So I was, thus, well supplied with raw materials for my artwork. I also found four hubcaps from a '50s-era Porsche, which I took back to Canada and sold.

Anyway, I was able to make three statues from the junk. One of them, "Bob," was perhaps two feet tall, a typical gringo tourist in a Chicago Bulls T-shirt, sneakers and shorts; he had a cloth bag over his shoulder and a line of zinc sunblock down his nose. He was a friendly, eager fellow, with his hand out, ready to shake and make friends. Another creature was called the *Monster Who Devoured D.F.* (distrito federal), who had a long vacuum-cleaner-hose nose. A third more resembled an escapee from the New Guinea highlands.

They were all accepted and displayed in the gallery.

I didn't get back to Oaxaca for several years. When I walked into La Mano Mágica, ready to give my excuse for this and that, the lady, upon seeing me, said, "Oh, I have some money for you."

The New Guinea–type figure had sold, the Monster was out on monthly loan, and Bob was in storage. A few days later, she had retrieved Bob and given him to me. I took him to the Portales and ordered a coffee. Bob was seated at the table with me. At the next table, I recognized the Canadian actress Jackie Burroughs. I introduced myself, and we all three became fast friends. In fact, Bob is still with Jackie, lo these many years later, living at her house outside Oaxaca, probably right now in his usual place in a niche looking out the window.*

*Alas, Jackie has died since the above was written.

TAKE 83

TICKET STUB FOR BASEBALL GAME; SEATTLE MARINERS VS. NEW YORK YANKEES, MAY 6, 1982, AT THE SEATTLE KINGDOME

I believe this was the night knuckleballer Nolan Ryan won his 300th game. But what I remember most was the bearded man with the U.S. Mail sack filled with triple-A batteries who was standing in one of the aisles in the bleachers along and above the left-field line. He was throwing the batteries into the crowd—and, of course, hitting people. I said, "Hey, man. What the hell are you doing?"

He replied, with a smile, "Oh, it's okay. I'm only throwing them in the nigger section."

TAKE 84

AN AD FOR THE CASTLE HAYMOUR IN PEACHLAND, BC

The ad shows a still photograph from an earlier movie entitled *Cleopatra* with Claudette Colbert and her Mark Antony, Henry Wilcoxon. As an aside here—and what is this entire book, if not an aside? But, then again, an aside to what?—I think this particular *Cleopatra* was a better movie than the more famous one that came twenty-some years later, with Taylor and Burton. The trouble with the latter one, besides the actors (Burton particularly), is the open vistas. When Claudette Colbert is carried through narrow, crowded streets, it seems more realistic than the vast, open spaces of the other movie. Wilcoxon, famous for giving the sermon in the bombed-out church at the end of Mrs. Miniver, looks like the kind of man who might conceivably rule an empire, unlike the other guy. By the way, there have been numerous movies about Cleopatra but only two other ones, as far as I know, called simply Cleopatra; the first in 1912, starred Helen Gardner, and the next, in 1917, with Theda Bara.

Above the photo is the line, "A Satisfied Couple in our Egyptian Room."

The Castle Haymour was a hotel built on the side of a hill by one Eddie Haymour. In addition to the Egyptian Room, guests could choose from other "Exotic Quarters": the Sultan Suite, Taj Mahal Room, Arabian Room, Roman Room and Queen of Sheba Suite.

Eddy Haymour was a Lebanese immigrant to Canada who had arrived in Edmonton in the late '50s with a piece of paper on which was written, "me, barber." I designed the ad while I was a sort of general factotum at the Castle.

Haymour had a remarkable history. In the early '70s, he had been thwarted in his attempts to build an Arab theme park on Rattlesnake Island in the Okanagan, and subjected to prison and the nuthouse. He returned to Lebanon and, with six of his cousins, everyone armed with Kalashnikov automatics, took the Canadian embassy hostage. Years later, I was enlisted by Canadian Business magazine to do a story about him. "He may be a dangerous nut," the editor told me. "Nobody else wants to try it." Well, I met Eddie Haymour and wrote a complimentary piece. He was very appreciative and eventually offered me the job of managing his hotel. Until that time, I had thought myself a good judge of character, not easy to fool, much less con. I should have listened to his second wife, Pat, who said, "Don't forget: whatever you're thinking, he's way ahead of you."

Haymour was a man who plotted every hour of every day of his life and probably never met a person he didn't try to best in one way or another.

And here I was working for the guy. It didn't end well. When I asked for back pay, he brought out his specially designed club, made from a two-by-four studded with spikes, and started swinging it at me (in the presence of his wife and nine-year-old daughter.) Fortunately, he was about as coordinated as he was truthful.

Anyway, I made that ad.

TAKE 85

LID OF THIN TIN CIGAR CASE

The box held small cigars made by the Dannemann company of São Félix, Bahia, in Brazil. I bought the cigars—what we'd call cigarillos—in the wild town of Benjamin Constant on the Amazon in Brazil. Funny and ironic that that muddy town of board sidewalks and muddy streets, where every other doorway led into a tavern or brothel, and with no signs of schools, churches or even civic buildings would be named after a French philosopher and educator.

It was my first trip to the Amazon, and I was just knocking around with no

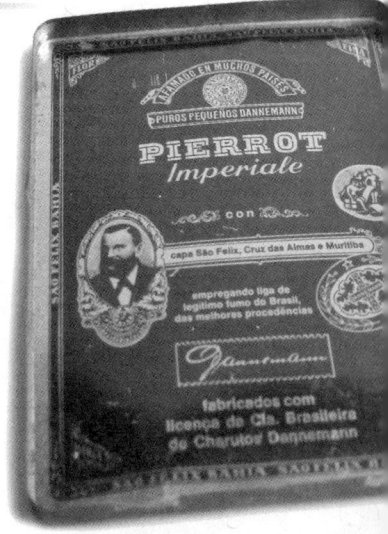

plan, going where the river took me. Of course, the Amazon itself is not always distinguishable from its competition: various channels, streams, creeks, and many a morass of swamp and devilish tunnels through the jungle known as *igarapes*.

Anyway, it is a beautiful tin lid; gold lettering on black, with a horizontal oval in which there is a portrait of Señor Dannemann framed by palm fronds and flanked by a wonderful riverfront scene complete with small sailboats, white buildings with red roofs and pale green hills in the background. Around the bottom of the portrait are colourful flowers and wooden boxes, presumably of cigars. The style of cigars is Pierrot Imperiale.

On the inside of the lid, the portrait is repeated, along with stamps and scroll work and the announcement, *"empregando liga de ligitimo funo do Brazil, das melhores procedencias."*

TAKE 86

A 50¢ PIECE FROM THE KINGDOM OF SWAZILAND

It was minted in 1974 and displays on its front a picture of King Sobhuza II, at the time the world's longest reigning monarch; on the back, an elephant and a lion flank a shield.

I was in Swaziland in 1978, resting and relaxing after covering conflicts in Namibia, Mozambique, and Rhodesia (as it was then called); I also spent two days in a sealed-off Soweto on the anniversary of the riots two years earlier.

So I was glad just to take it easy. At the bar of the Highland Village Motel, I shared a drink or two with Mr. Swaziland, the country's leading bodybuilder. We got along so well that he invited me to train with him the day after tomorrow. I agreed,

thinking it was just barroom talk. He said that a car would come by for me in the morning.

It did—a limousine—and it delivered me and my new friend to the palace of King Sobhuza II. The entrance to the palace was guarded by a pair of male lions. My friend said, "It's the females you have to watch out for."

"Ain't that always the way it is," I couldn't help replying.

I got a good look at the old king when he walked across the hallway. He was wearing sandals, a dashiki and a white-lined jacket. He said something to my companion in Swahili, and smiled and greeted me.

It seemed that the king was so grateful to my companion for spreading news about their country throughout the world that he had had a small workout facility built for him in the palace. The only awkward moment of the experience was when we actually began exercising. The man was a monster, his arms like bowling balls. I considered myself a sturdy fellow but felt like a geek next to him. Whatever body part he exercised, I made sure to work on one as far away as possible. When, for instance, he worked his trapezius, I worked my calves.

Later, I took a short stroll around the grounds of the place. Everyone was as friendly as could be. Now, it all seems like a dream.

Of course, so many of the memories provoked by going through this tin box of mine seem like dreams. Maybe it could be thought of as a dream box.

TAKE 87

A RESTAURANT PLACEMAT, A BUSINESS CARD, AND AN ITEM FROM BC BOOKWORLD

The restaurant placemat gives information about inventions. It's labelled "inventions through the ages." The ones featured are the wheel, the light bulb, the phonograph, the camera, the telephone, the clock and the steam engine. There is a drawing of, and information about, each invention. For instance, of the clock, we learn, "One of the earliest timepieces was the sundial. Next came the hourglass and an early Greek water clock called the Clepsydra. In the 13th century, mechanical clocks were built using weight, wheels and gears to turn the hands of the dial. The first pocket watches were made possible in the 15th century by the invention of the mainspring. In the 1650s, a Dutch scientist named Christiaan Huygens designed a clock with a pendulum."

I must have saved this paper placemat during the months I was working for the company mentioned on the business card, Inventex. The company was a division of a development company. The people were all serious business types who thought there was money to be made on inventions. At the time, there was no company that would work with an inventor to help develop his or her brainchild from a sketch of a rough model through patent search and research and development, and then to market. Most companies bought an invention outright (or stole it). Not many basement tinkerers can even afford a patent search.

I came into the picture because it became apparent to the capitalists that they were constitutionally incapable of having anything to do with the inventors, nor did they want to. They didn't understand the inventors, and it was invariably the case that they looked down on them. The inventors were perplexed by the business types and afraid, justifiably, of being hornswoggled. So I got the job of intermediary. I'd find the inventors, talk to them and report back to the businessmen.

Which leads to the small item about George Knap, published in BC BookWorld. This appeared several years after I'd heard about George, met with him in a doughnut shop in Burnaby, gone to see his spaceship and reported to the company.

Here are the contents of the BookWorld item:

"Whereas most writers only receive rejection letters from publishers, George Knap of Burnaby has rejection letters from NASA, Canadian astronaut Marc Garneau and U.S. Senator John Glenn.

"Knap, an inventor, has reprinted much of his correspondence in a self-published memoir, Spaceship Conspiracy ... Knap claims there's been a conspiracy between the Canadian and American governments to suppress his 'orbital propulsion' invention, for which he received a U.S. patent in 1978.

"Knap's memoir is subtitled The True Story of the Inventor of Orbital Propulsion Powered Spaceships and his Fight for Recognition.

"With a grade eight formal education, Knap says he has invented more than 200 items since 1941, but has yet to make a

penny. He conceived of orbital propulsion one day in his living room. 'This type of orbital propulsion spaceship would be able to take off from any suitable airport, where it could fly directly to other planets or star systems at maximum speed and return to earth the same way.'"

I'd heard about Knap, and when I took this job in 1987, I gave him a call. I took along a fellow from Inventex, the most casual and friendly of the bunch. No sooner had we sat down than Knap began telling us that his spaceship was capable of getting to the moon in a matter of three or four days, and that he would drive it himself were he a tad more nimble. All the time Knap talked, one of his eyes remained fixed on us while the other roamed around the room. The man from Inventex hung in for about five minutes before spinning around on his stool and making for the exit, having suddenly remembered that he had an important engagement on the other side of Vancouver.

Knap and I talked for twenty minutes, and then I left with him for his house. It was a small two-bedroom detached home like all the others in the area. We conducted our business in the kitchen. On the refrigerator door were charts and formulae on graph paper held in place by magnets; on the table: books, manuals, more paper amidst coffee cups, saucers, bowls and empty cans.

He told me that he already had the patent for his spaceship and all he wanted us for was to be his agent, to secure the use of an airport, promote his venture, and make him lots of money.

"And where is your spaceship right now?" I pictured it under wraps at a local airport; Chilliwack, perhaps, or Abbotsford.

Knap pointed out his kitchen window.

"In the yard. Back by the laneway."

We went out to look at it. There was some tarnished metal out there that looked like a large propane tank but no spaceship that I could see.

"Where is it, in back of the garage?"

"No, that's it, right there."

"Oh."

It was lying on the lawn, about ten feet long and tapered to a point, with three flanges or wings at the other end. It would have been difficult to get a pilot in there or electronic equipment in lieu of a pilot.

"You sure it'll make it to the moon, eh?"

"No problem," declared Mr. Knap.

TAKE 88

NEWS CLIPPING, PROBABLY FROM THE SEATTLE POST-INTELLIGENCER, EARLY 1980S: "NEW YAKIMA GADGET HARNESSES WOMANPOWER"

Below the headline is a photograph of a farm contraption with a long gantry arm from which hang several women in harnesses; they are suspended a couple of feet over farm fields. A cutline below the photo reads, "Diana Brooks of Prosser, Benton County, hangs suspended in the air as she cuts an asparagus stalk at the Yakima Chief Ranches."

This reminds me very much of some collage done by surrealists—*not them again!*—but it is not surreal; it is real. It's a little picture from life, as weird and surprising as life.

TAKE 89

CARDBOARD FOLDER WITH METAL ADDRESSOGRAPH INSIDE. IT IS A "SERVICE FEE RECORD" AND IDENTIFIES ONE JAMES R. CHRISTY AS A MEMBER OF THE NATIONAL MARITIME UNION OF AMERICA, AFL-CIO. ON THE INSIDE FRONT PAGE IS A HEAD-AND-SHOULDERS SHOT OF THE FELLOW LOOKING IMPOSSIBLY YOUNG. HE WAS BORN IN VIRGINIA AND SHIPPED OUT ONE TIME ONLY, ON 6-16-66.

4" X 6" COLOUR PHOTOGRAPH OF AN ASSEMBLAGE BY ME

It shows old radio parts, a toxic-looking tree cut from plywood, a basketball player cut from plywood, oil-tanker trucks, tin tubing, plastic and metal odds and ends, and standing above all this is a carved and painted figure that looks like a cross between a mafia don and a business mogul of the old school. I don't remember the title of the piece, but it probably has something to do with New Jersey; it reminds me of New Jersey. The backdrop to the assemblage is a quilted green sleeping bag.

TAKE 91

ESSAY FROM B.C. HISTORICAL NEWS—SUMMER 1997, TITLED "THE PROSTITUTION OF NATIVE WOMEN ON THE NORTH COAST OF BRITISH COLUMBIA," BY JENNIFER WINDECKER

Unfortunately, the first column of the first page, page 29, of this essay is missing, as are the last one or two pages, succeeding page 32. Windecker, in column two, page 29, quotes a historian named Carol Cooper, that "there was little evidence of prostitution, as defined by European standards, in these aboriginal societies prior to contact with Whites," then goes on to unwittingly contradict that statement, while seeming to concur: "The sexuality of some Native women was utilized as a form of social and economic transaction" (prior to contact with whites.)

An interesting article, and I regret not having it in its entirety. Why I have it at all, I'm not sure. It may have seemed relevant to a writing project I had begun for a book on British Columbia. That book never worked out due to a conflict I had with the publisher in regard to direction. I didn't want to turn out a goody-two-shoes tome featuring wise old salts, crusty poetry-spouting loggers, dignified native persons and breathtaking vistas, at least not exclusively.

TAKE 92

PICTURE POSTCARD FEATURING A BLACK AND WHITE PHOTOGRAPH OF THE IMMORTAL LESTER YOUNG, IN PORKPIE HAT AND PINSTRIPED SUIT, SITTING ON A CHAIR WITH HIS TENOR SAXOPHONE ACROSS HIS KNEES

He's looking up in the direction of the ceiling or the angels beyond with his big, sad eyes. When he played, he lagged along behind the beat. He was nicknamed "Pres"—the President of the saxophone—but to me he was the greatest, more like God. The purest poet. He seemed to take off, go somewhere else when he was playing; he himself stayed on the ground, perhaps, but his music levitated. Very few artists lift off like that, hardly any writers, some singers: Caruso and Beniamino Gigli, for instance.

I revere the man above all other artists.

TAKE 93

LOS ANGELES TIMES' STORY BY HENRY CHU, PRINTED IN THE VANCOUVER SUN, SOMETIME IN AUTUMN OF 2004

The story marks the death in Jiangyong County, Hunan province, China, of Yang Huanyi, "the last surviving writer and speaker of an enigmatic language invented and used only by women in a small pocket of central China."

It seems that Yang and her contemporaries had inherited the language, known as *nushu*, from their mothers and grandmothers. "Confined to home, the women of Jiangyong traded gossip, spread news and lamented their lot in letters, poems and songs that they collected in books, embroidered into handkerchiefs and painted on fans."

The language's origins remain unclear, but the word *nushu* means "woman's script" in Chinese. There is only one line in Chu's article that indicates the purpose of the language, a means of communication developed so that women could "share their joys and sorrows, hopes and fears, away from the prying eyes of men."

Chinese Communist authorities denounced the language in the late '60s as a feudal leftover, and they destroyed many *nushu* texts.

Yang Huanyi, according to the writer, was stooped with age at the end of her life, "her face wizened, her hair and teeth nearly gone."

Now by a strange coincidence—but then most coincidences are strange—just prior to dipping into my Sweet Assorted tin box, I had been reading Eduardo Galeano's latest book, *Mirrors,* and on page 29 came upon his own story of Yang Huanyi, "the last to know *nushu.*"

The Uruguayan author says that *nushu* was an alphabet of symbols "that masqueraded as decorations and was indecipherable to the eyes of their masters."

The women, he said, sketched their words on garments and fans. "The hands that embroidered were not free. The symbols were."

Now Chu points out that *nushu* symbols were loose and flowing, and bore no resemblance to the boxy complex Chinese characters. Loose and flowing, they could easily pass as abstract decoration. If the idea behind the language was to have a means of communication that was not comprehensible to men, why would women compile books of writings, which would be noticed by men, destroyed and forbidden?

Galeano notes that Yang Huanyi's feet were crippled and that she "stumbled through life." He doesn't say that her feet had been bound in keeping with that particular male fetish and to keep women from wandering and getting into trouble. He doesn't say it but implies it, as his story on Yang Huanyi comes immediately after one called "Foot Murderers."

TAKE 94

KODACHROME SLIDE, OR TRANSPARENCY, OF GENE CARSEY AND FRIEND, AT CARSEY'S FUNNY FARM IN BEND, OREGON

I found Gene's forty acres in the course of my searches for unusual homes and gardens. For years, I sought out places, homes and gardens that people had personalized in a bizarre manner. I still do this but mainly now in other countries. In North America, as I pointed out in a book called *Strange Sites*, not many of these places exist anymore. First of all, there are fewer people around with the kind  of all-around skills required to build them. Second, land is getting too expensive. Third, building regulations and zoning laws mitigate against this kind of exuberant free expression. If I want to build a bottle house on my own property, why can't I?

Gene Carsey didn't build any bottle houses but he planted a bowling-ball garden and dug a love canal.

I'd heard there was a man by that name doing strange things on forty acres near Bend, Oregon. I phoned the only Carsey in the Bend, Oregon, phone book. The woman who answered told me that Gene didn't live there.

"Are you related?"

"I'm afraid so," she said. "He's my son."

I got his unlisted number and called him. Gene gave me directions: "Turn right down the dirt trail when you get to the bowling-ball garden."

"Okay. See you soon." I replied casually, wanting him to think bowling-ball gardens and me go way back.

I turned right, as directed, drove on up past the bowling balls on stakes, saw the Love Canal in the distance, and parked close to the ant farm. There was a house with a Newfoundland dog on the roof.

Carsey was a husky, big-handed fellow who'd gotten his property and simply did what he wanted with it, and what he wanted to do was let his imagination run free.

The authorities hadn't wanted him to let his imagination run free, at least not in the direction where it headed. "They told me I couldn't do this kind of thing unless I was a farm. When I asked what I needed to be considered a farm, they told me animals. So I got animals."

Besides ants, he got cats, dogs, a couple of pigs, other animals that were missing limbs or were blind, and plenty of goats—fainting goats. If you kept your gaze long enough on the goat pasture over near the Love Canal, you'd see a goat just topple over, stay that way for several minutes, then get up again.

The Love Canal was a pool in the shape of a valentine with an arrow piercing it from above. Couples went there to get married or have their wedding receptions by the side of the canal. The rentals and a junk shop kept the place going.

He was a nice man, Gene. I took this picture of him and his buddy, Mike.

Although I visited the farm three or four times, I haven't been back in years. So many of these places come to bad ends. I'm almost afraid to know what has happened to it.

TAKE 95

CLIPPING FROM THE GLOBE AND MAIL

For many years, at the back of the *Globe and Mail*, there has been a Social Studies section, a miscellany of information. I clipped a notice from it called "Robotic Park." I was going to write that I did this five or six years ago, but I see on the back of the item an advertisement for a 2002 Cadillac, which means that it must have been 2001 when I found the piece. It is about a robot that escaped. I wrote a poem about the robot, named Gaak, in the story.

Gaak Busts Out
Real name Gaak, two feet
Tall, split from the Centre
In Rotterham. He'd rather
Be somewhere else, anywhere,
On the Outside. This two-fanged
Predator sucked power from less
Nimble prey, when he could find
Some. What else was there
To do? His captors turned their
Backs and Gaak was gone; crept
The wall and found a gap, cool
As Cagney, and lammed it. Trundled
Down a truck ramp and made
For the parking lot, where they
Nabbed him. Gaak going round
And round and round on asphalt

In a chirascuro pirouette,
Solar batteries foiled by light
And leaves. "It's fantastic,
Yeah," said one of his warders.
"But him and his kind won't
Be taking over
Just yet."

The guy really said that: Professor Noel Sharkey, "robotic expert,"
University of Sheffield.

TAKE 96

YELLOW-GREEN PLASTIC SOLDIER,
THREE INCHES HIGH, WEARING
HELMET, RIGHT LEG RAISED
AS IF HE'S RUNNING; RIGHT
HAND HOLDING A RIFLE;
LEFT ARM RAISED

In a hurry to
be a hero, or
a statistic.

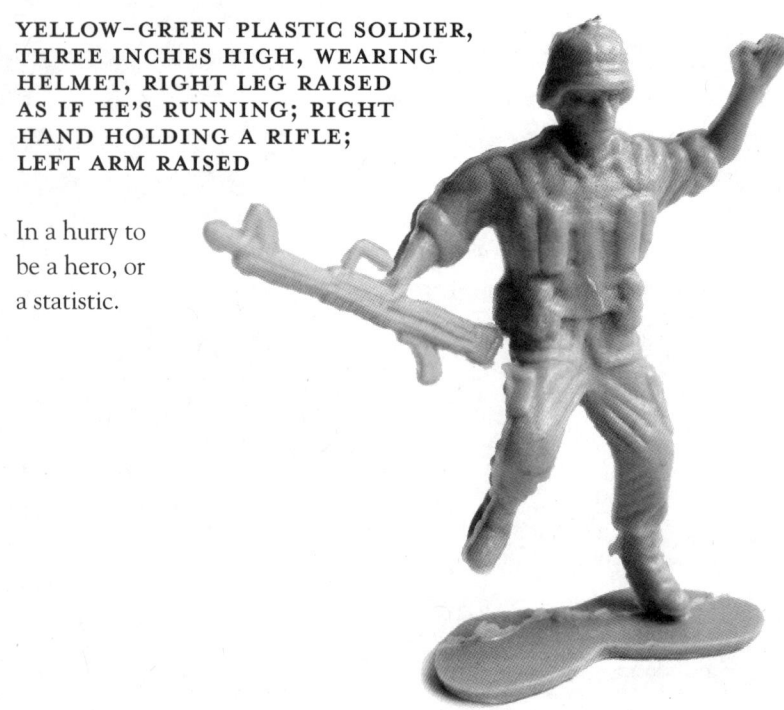

TAKE 97

NEWSPAPER STORY ABOUT HARLEIGH CEMETERY, CAMDEN, NEW JERSEY; FROM THE PHILADELPHIA INQUIRER; DON'T KNOW THE DATE

Harleigh Cemetery in Camden County. Walt Whitman is buried there. There is a photograph of his tomb: it's in the background; in the foreground is the cemetery administrator Bob Smyth. He's posed near a thick-trunked birch tree, carved with graffiti that consists mostly of initials, except one joker has formed the word DIE.

Also buried there is "Civil War hero and U.S. Sen. William Joyce." In fact, he is mentioned in the article before the good grey poet. Also in attendance is Nicholas A. Virgilio, "a Camden poet and internationally recognized author of haiku." He, too, gets more space than Whitman. There is a tradition in the area of ignoring or slighting Walt Whitman, he being a disreputable character. One of the bridges between Philadelphia and Camden, where Walt had his last residence, is named for him. But it was quite a struggle to get that approved. After all, he is the author of such lines as "All is lacking if sex is lacking."

During a debate over the naming of the bridge, one ward leader rose and declared, "We can't name a bridge after no fruitcake."

My parents lived in an apartment in Collingswood, where the cemetery is located. From their kitchen window one could almost see Walt's mausoleum. It's on Haddon Avenue, across the street from a hospital, beyond which are streets of stripped-down cars, broken glass and crack houses: the City of Camden, annual U.S. winner of the distinction of Highest Crime Rate.

Ah, Walt. Such is your democratic vista now.

TAKE 98

BLACK-AND-WHITE PHOTOGRAPH OF FRONT SIDE OF THIS SWEET ASSORTED BOX: "FAMOUS ENGLISH BISCUITS"

Why did I take a photo of the box and put it inside this box and not some other box, or slip it in a pocket or stick it in a drawer? That way at least if I ever lost the box, I'd have the photo to remember it by. Beats me.

TAKE 99

SHEET OF WHITE, LEGAL-SIZE PAPER, FOLDED IN HALF WITH SKETCHES IN FINE-LINE, BLACK MAGIC MARKER

It's folded horizontally with drawings mostly on one side. There is a sketch of four figures, all vaguely human. They are at work, because one is carrying a lunch bucket and there's a clock on the wall. Perhaps they work at a nuclear plant, because there is a window near the clock through which can be seen what look like three reactors. I suppose this was a sketch for a painting never done; perhaps the figures "in real life" started as human, but the effects of their drudgery—and radiation—have made them less so. The guy on the right reminds me somewhat of Woody Guthrie.

Below this sketch is one of an armless female figure on a stand. Her head is meant to be a pot lid; she has a hat that might be half of a globe of the world.

This is a sketch for a sculpture called Ms. *I Been Everywhere*. I made a Mr. *I Been Everywhere* and thought he needed a wife. He sold, and so I made *The Second Mr. I Been Everywhere*. Him, I traded to Joe Ferone for an electric keyboard. Ms. *I Been Everywhere* was thus alone again but sold before a third husband appeared.

TAKE 100

TWO PAGES OF WHITE LEGAL-SIZE PAPER WITH TYPEWRITER TYPING, CORRECTIONS AND ADDITIONS IN BLACK INK, WORDS AND LINES CROSSED OUT WITH GREEN MAGIC MARKER

I was writing about British Columbia; it didn't work out, as mentioned in Take 91. These two pages are all I have left of the manuscript. The writing ends in the middle of a line.

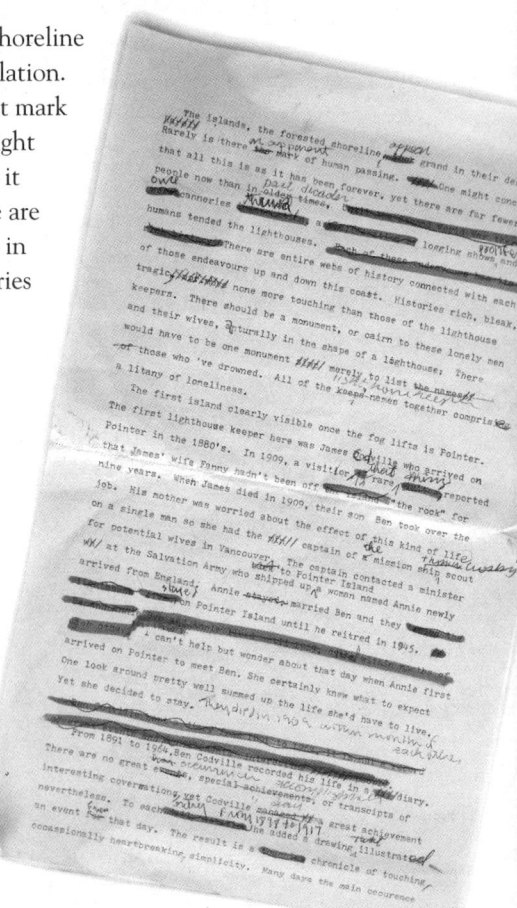

The islands, the forested shoreline appear grand in their desolation. Rarely is there an apparent mark of human passing. One might conclude that all this is as it has been forever, yet there are far fewer people now than in past decades. Once canneries thrived, logging shows proliferated and humans tended the lighthouses. There are entire webs of history connected with each of those endeavours up and down the coast. Histories rich, bleak, tragic; none more touching than those of the lighthouse keepers. There should be a monument or cairn to these lonely men and their wives, naturally in the shape of a lighthouse. There would have to be one monument merely to list those who've drowned. All of the lighthouse keepers names together comprise a litany of loneliness.

The first island clearly visible once the fog lifts is Pointer. *[Note: I was riding the ferry up to Prince Rupert from Port Hardy.]* The first lighthouse keeper here was James Codville, who arrived on Pointer in the 1880s. In 1909, a visitor, that rare thing, reported that James's wife Fanny hadn't been off "the rock" for nine years. When James died in 1909, their son Ben took over the job. His mother was worried about the effect of this kind of life on a single man, so she had the captain of the mission ship scout for potential wives in Vancouver. The captain contacted a minister at the Salvation Army, who whipped up to Pointer Island a woman named Annie, newly arrived from England. Annie married Ben, and they stayed on Pointer Island until he retired in 1945.

I can't help but wonder about that day when Annie first arrived on Pointer to meet Ben. She certainly knew immediately what to expect. One look around pretty well summed up the life she'd have to live. Yet she decided to stay. They died in 1969 within a month of each other.

From 1891 to 1964, Ben Codville recorded his life in a diary. There are no great occurrences, special occurrences or accomplishments, or transcripts of interesting conversations, yet Codville's diary is a great achievement nevertheless. To each entry from 1898 to 1917, he added a drawing that illustrated an event from that day. The result is a chronicle of touching, occasionally heartbreaking simplicity. Many days, the main occurrence is the sight of a canoe, a sailboat or a line of ducks. These Ben would draw, and title: "Ducks Passed," "Tug Passed." Other pictures are labelled "Whale" and "Poppys in Bloom." One August 11th, he drew his woodshed, but the next day produced "Cat on Woodshed." The busiest and, consequently, happiest drawings are ones crammed with newspapers and envelopes of all size; even the cancellation marks on the stamps are done with care; these drawings are titled "MAIL."

I took a seat at the very front of the ship, to read and watch the prow cleave the grey water. There was a woman to my right who worked for a tour company as a guide. She was furiously scribbling "thank you" cards to participants of the last Inside Passage tour; furiously, because, as she said, she only had ten minutes before returning to her current group, currently distracted in the cafeteria.

To my left, a few seats away, was a man I immediately thought I knew from somewhere. Just as I was about to say something, he pulled a book from his cloth bag. Seeing that it was a German language guide to B.C., I assumed I was wrong.

Outside were so many islands, hills, rounded mountains, and jagged mountains that I thought of old stage machinery being pulled back and forth with pulleys and rollers.

I ignored my book to eavesdrop on some retired people behind me, residents of Canada, part of a tour but not that being conducted by the lady beside me. I heard one man ask another man about the war. "I was with the Canadian infantry," he said. "How about you?"

This man rather shyly admitted serving in the German army.

"Well, it was long ago," said the man born in Canada, adding pointedly, "though some people have long memories."

"Yes," said the German. "I was captured by the Americans and held prisoner for a few years. Afterwards, I could find no work in Germany but was unable to emigrate."

"Yeah? So what did you do?"

"I joined the French Foreign Legion."

I turned around at that, as if casually wondering where that wife of mine had gotten to, and hazarded a glance at him. A seventy-five-year-old German man in a...

That's where my two legal-size pages end.

I don't have the rest of the manuscript, which must have run to 400 typewritten pages. What happened to this manuscript (which was about British Columbia now and then, a sort of travel/history/reportage), I have no idea. Maybe it is in a forgotten storage bin or resides in another tin box or a battered suitcase somewhere.

But I know that soon after listening to the conversation between the two old soldiers, I went to the cafeteria, and while having a coffee, saw the younger German man with the guidebook. I happened to look up, and he was looking at me quizzically. I went over and asked if we knew each other, and as I did that, we both simultaneously realized where we had met.

It was two years earlier in Puerto Escondido, Mexico. A friend and I were having a meal in a seafood restaurant on the waterfront. We began a conversation with another couple, Germans. When they found out that we were from British Columbia they began plying us with questions about the province. Western Canada is immensely attractive to Germans. I once went to locate what remained of a place called Grand Forks in the Yukon, in what they call the Klondike. During the Gold Rush days, Grand Forks arose and flourished as sort of a satellite town to Dawson City. There were more than ten thousand people living there by 1899, yet even most Yukoners don't know that it ever existed. It was a long and arduous hike from the gravel road, but when I got to the site many years ago, there were three Germans there and they knew all about it.

Anyway, this man and woman said they wanted very much to go to British Columbia, and they asked us what they should see and do. He was a medical doctor involved in research; she might also have been a doctor; I don't remember, but it's all in my lost manuscript. I do recall that they told me they spent their spare time hiking and reading about Indians and outdoors lore. I told them that if they went to British Columbia, they must certainly go to northern Vancouver Island and take the ferry from Port Hardy to Prince Rupert. Don't take a cruise ship, I said, but the B.C. ferry.

And here he was, on the B.C. ferry.

"Yes, I wrote it down, what you said. When I get to Prince Rupert, I will take the train east to this place Prince George, which you also told me to do."

"And don't forget when you get to Prince George, you should ride the B.C. Rail train down to North Vancouver."

"And then I will go to the Okanagan."

"Where is your lady friend, or was she your wife?"

"She was my wife. We are no longer together. And what about your lady friend or your wife?"

"My lady friend. We're not together either."

"Such is the way."

TAKE 101

NOTEPAD WITH FOUR PAGES REMAINING. FROM MEIKLES HOTELS RHODESIA, PO BOX 594, SALISBURY, RHODESIA. ABOVE THE NAME AND ADDRESS IS A CROWN FORMED LIKE AN "M" NESTLED IN A BOWL MADE OF TWO PEN STROKES. THIS IS IN DARK RED.

I went to Africa in the '70s to cover conflicts in Rhodesia, as it was called, and in Namibia and Mozambique, and I smuggled myself into Soweto when it was closed to people who didn't live there. In between forays into the countryside in Rhodesia, I repaired to Salisbury and stayed at the Meikles Hotel. As far as I could tell, the other journalists rarely left the hotel unless it was to troop over to the Ministry of Information, where they received handouts from Colonel Gates, the Minister's press liaison. Then the journalists—and I'm talking about representatives of big, highly respected newspapers and news organizations—rewrote the reports from their predominately mild-leftist perspective. They spiced these up with quotes from "a source close to the guerilla forces," these being the black men in white, starched uniforms who served them drinks in the lobby of the Meikles.

I was the first outsider at the Umtali Massacre at the mission school in the Mountains of the Moon, up near the Mozambique border. I was there all day but never saw any other westerners, except dead teachers and their families. The massacre was the work of Mugabe's forces, who, before hacking those people to death, delivered a political speech to the young black students. The kids were told that education just played into the hands of the whites. The students watched their teachers and their families die. Children first.

I got a ride out of there with a black Rhodesian soldier. We were ambushed on the road by guerillas but rescued, eventually, by Rhodesian soldiers on curfew patrol. The car, a Ford Anglia, looked like a colander when the shooting was done.

A couple of days later, the television crews arrived at Meikles, and the brave journalists chartered a plane to take them to the mission school.

My story reported the facts, but I also offered the opinion that it was important to note that the situation in Rhodesia bore no resemblance to that in South Africa, that Robert Mugabe was evil and, should he seize power, there would be hell to pay. This was in 1978, and I don't hesitate to state that I was right.

When I got back to Toronto, however, and called at the offices of *Weekend Magazine* that had sent me to Africa, I found that the chief editor, Peter Sympnowich, had changed my copy and given the article an entirely different slant. He obliterated any mark of Mugabe's hand on the massacre. Suddenly, it became the work of unknown assailants. The way the piece stood when I saw it—in proofs, fortunately—had been transformed into typical jerk-off liberal, pro-Mugabe, anti-Ian Smith nonsense.

No sooner had I read the piece handed to me by Senior Editor Gary Ross than I saw Sympnowich on the other side of the floor. I went after him. He saw me, rushed into his office and locked the door. He didn't have the courage to confront me; he simply cowered in there. I shouted predictable things but also informed him that he was so stupid that he had illustrated the piece with photographs from South Africa, mainly South African cops holding Alsatian dogs, straining at their leashes a couple of feet from small black children.

And Gary Ross had the great moral courage to say to me, patronizingly, "And how long were you in Rhodesia, Jim?"

"Three weeks."

And he smirked as if to say, well, what can you expect to have learned in that short of a time? I replied, "How long were you in Rhodesia, Gary? And your poltroon of a boss? Or anyone else here?"

I threatened a lawsuit. The article was changed but still was not as powerful as I had first written it. Nor did they use any pictures from the several roles of film that I gave them; nor did I ever receive the film back.

After the story appeared, there were letters to the editor denouncing me as racist and a "right-wing fanatic." This was particularly pleasing, because the week before the Rhodesia piece came out, *Weekend* published my story about being in a closed-down Soweto on the second anniversary of the 1976 riot. That story provoked letters calling me "a Commie dupe." Some of these letters appeared in the same issue.

TAKE 102

RECEIPT ON BLUE PAPER FROM THE OTTAWA Y.M./Y.W.C.A., MADE OUT TO ME, RESIDENT OF 77 FLORENCE STREET

On January 24, 1969, I paid $18 to take a basic photography course. I learned composition and how to develop and print photographs. I used a thirty-five millimetre camera bought at a pawn shop in Bytown. I've never really expanded—developed!—these photography skills, although I have, over the years, published dozens of images, and not just to accompany my own articles. Years ago, I even sold some shots of Greenland to an agency. I had a photograph of the Yukon published in a magazine in Thailand and a couple of golf photos in a newspaper in the Northwest Territories.

But all this was just by happenstance. I don't really like to take photographs, unless it's all agreed upon, like with the golf story, or when it's a landscape shot and no one's around. I don't like to be seen with the camera or to put the camera between me and what I'm looking at. That said, I have dozens of photographs I've taken around the world of handmade signs.

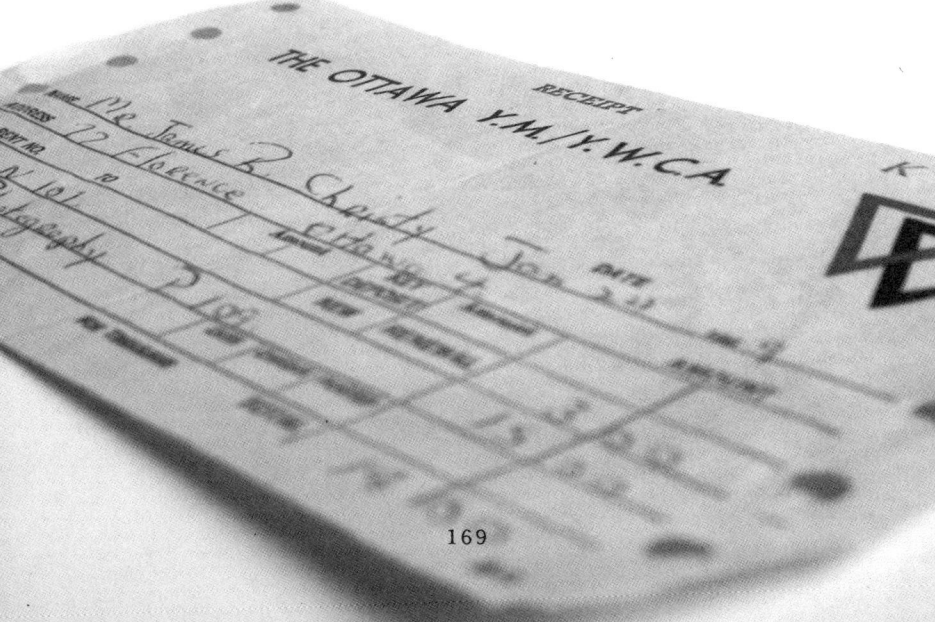

TAKE 103

NOTE WRITTEN TO ME WITH A BLACK BALLPOINT PEN ON A STRIP OF WHITE PAPER, THE REVERSE SIDE OF A BCSPCA PAD. ON THE BUSINESS SIDE ARE PICTURES OF A PUPPY AND A CAT, WITH THE LEGEND "SPEAKING FOR ANIMALS."

The note reads, "Jim: How's the cleanup going? If you have time for a break consider my place tonight (Mon) say 7 pm—Al is on board & I'll try to get others—maybe Robt + Pete… or Tues aft. If that's better. Stu 6-____."

I was living on the Sunshine Coast of B.C. and this note probably dates from when I was getting ready to move east. At least, I figure that explains the "cleanup." I had a trailer and was cleaning it out, prior to putting it on the market. It would have been 2005 or 2006. "Al" is Al Maclachlan, a musician and cameraman, author of two novels: *After the Funeral* and *Murmurs of the Dead*; "Robt," is Robert Kinnard, a painter; "Pete," is Peter Trower, the poet; "Stu," Stuart Young, a musician. Only Stu still lives in Gibsons.

I live on the other side of the country now, and those people and that place seem like part of another lifetime, even though I see Robert Kinnard and Al Maclachlan every couple of years. The former is one of the best painters I've ever met, but he doesn't play the art-world game, doesn't do the networking and bullshitting that seem to be a part of it. Same with Al Maclachlan. With his various talents, he should be famous or at least make some money at what he does. But, no; he can't talk the talk anymore than Kinnard is able to compose the required Artist's Statement. At least Pete Trower is old enough to be entrenched as a legend on the Coast and Stu Young has a regular job.

As for the place, it was at one time a haven for people like that and all manner of drifters and rapscallions, lamsters and remittance men. Now, it's a paradise for retirees and *le haute bourgeoisie* people from the city, half of them opening bed-and-breakfast joints to cater to people just like themselves who haven't bought property yet but who come to look around. But enough of them have bought property that real estate is far beyond the reach of the types of people mentioned above, as well as the loggers and fishers, who made the place interesting in the first place. Every time I go back there, which isn't often, I get many people saying to me, "Aren't you sorry you moved away from Paradise?" No.

TAKE 104

INVITATION TO AN ART OPENING AND VERNISSAGE ON DONDERDAG 13 MAART 2003, AT THE ZEDES ART GALLERY, 36 RUE PAUL LAUTERS—1050, BRUXELLES

The show is of paintings by Martin Vaughn-James, whom I met in 1970 in Toronto. He later moved to Paris with his partner, Sarah McCoy. I visited them there in 1984. A few years later, they moved to Brussels.

Back in 1970, Martin was already doing what came to be called graphic novels. He had some success with a book called *The Cage*. We would sit around their apartment near Casa Loma discussing surrealism and Lautremont. They were very smart and a lot of fun; those were good days. Unfortunately, we lost track of each other after 1984.

TAKE 105

SMALL, TORN PIECE OF PAPER WITH TWO SKETCHES AND HALF OF A NAME AND PHONE NUMBER

At the bottom left, I've drawn, in blue ink, a guy with a piggy nose wearing a crown. Next to him, in black ink, is half of some kind of pod or space vehicle with plants growing out of the ports. On the other side of this piece of paper, not in my handwriting, are some parts of names and notations. For instance, one is "…nitty Chimney—$100 for repai…" Another is "Lisa …48 …66"

These notes would be from 2008–2009.

I have not one idea what this is about. Maybe it's a receipt. I like to think it indicates that one Nitty Chimney paid one Repai $100. And 48 and 66 are the second and third of Lisa's measurements (although on second thought, I hope not).

TAKE 106

CLIPPING FROM VANCOUVER SUN FROM 1987 ABOUT SOMEONE I'LL CALL RICHARD CHARTOFF: "CANOE TRIPPER RUNS AFOUL OF EXPO WITH PACIFIC SCHEME"

It seems that "Richard Chartoff," who said he planned to sail an outrigger crew from a certain island in Micronesia to Vancouver in time for Expo '86, was using the proposed trip and the publicity it was sure to engender to tout a hotel scheme he had for that certain island. Expo spokesperson Gail Flitton is quoted as saying that Expo had endorsed the voyage by including it in the "specialized periods program" but stressed that did not allow Chartoff to use the Expo logo.

The reason I have the clipping is because I had the misfortune to get involved with Richard Chartoff. I can't remember our first meeting but I know he contacted me because of publicity surrounding a recent adventure of my own. I had found a buried city in the jungle of Central America. I was on several radio programs, got written up in the business section of the *Globe and Mail* and in the *National Enquirer*. Soon we were meeting and discussing plans to captain a traditional eighty-foot-long baurua outrigger. Chartoff claimed to have lots of experience along these lines. Whatever doubts I had about that were allayed by the fact that we'd have a crew of locals doing the work and, as for the boat, it was twice as long as either the *Nina*, *Pinta* or *Santa Maria*, and more seaworthy. This would be the trip from Micronesia to Vancouver later mentioned in the newspaper article.

Richard Chartoff was short and wiry, with close-cropped hair and a moustache. He talked a mile a minute and was filled with ideas. I thought he seemed a tad less than robust, but when we erected a radio tower on top of a building on Homer Street, he scurried up to the top with agility and without fear.

Some of his claims made me skeptical, but he had been to that Micronesian island, had dozens of photographs and had met the King. In fact, one day we telephoned the king at his compound and

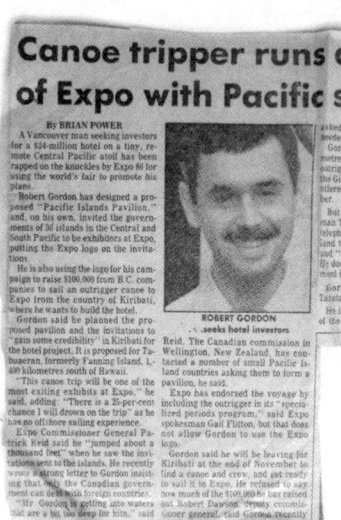

actually got through. I told the man I was honoured to talk to him on the phone and looked forward to meeting him in person. Seemed like a nice enough fellow.

My involvement with Chartoff and the trip ended on the evening before Expo officially opened. We were invited to a speech given by Thor Heyerdahl, who first gained fame by taking a reed boat across the Pacific to prove that Polynesians could sail long distances in ancient times. He went on to make other archaeological discoveries throughout the world. Afterwards, we met the great man, and Chartoff outlined his navigation plans. I distinctly remember the look in Heyerdahl's eyes when he told us, politely, that the trip was impossible, given the currents.

As we made our way from the building later that evening, I said, "Well, we have to rethink our route."

"Oh, Heyerdahl," Chartoff replied. "What does he know!"

That was it for me.

It was not long after, that I saw the story in the *Sun*. Chartoff had talked about a hotel being part of his long-range plans to settle in the South Pacific, but I hadn't known that he was using the Expo logo or claiming that they were sponsoring him.

I ran into Richard Chartoff five years later, working as a clerk at the registration desk at an Inn on Georgia Street in Vancouver. He promptly informed me that he was the Messiah but was having a difficult time convincing people, even though he was half-Jewish and it had been written that when Jesus re-appeared, he would be recognized because he was half-Jewish.

TAKE 107

BUSINESS CARD FOR JIM JOHNSTON AND HIS COUNT 10 PRODUCTIONS

Known as J.J., Jim Johnston was a boxing manager, agent and would-be promoter. Tall and gaunt, with a devilish glint in his eye, he was a great storyteller and not reluctant to be both hero and joker of his tales.

One time, having received a telephone call from a matchmaker in South Africa, J.J. assured the man that he did indeed have a heavyweight fighter with a respectable record, no rising star but no tomato can either. Well, he didn't have a heavyweight that fit that description—but he did have a middleweight.

"But how did you figure on getting a middleweight past the promoters? What about the weigh-in?"

Such concerns never impeded J.J. as he went about his business. He was not going to let a small matter of thirty pounds keep him from getting a free trip to Johannesburg. He took his fighter. (I won't mention his name, or rather his nickname, which is what he fought under, but he met two of the matchmaker's requirements: he was neither rising star nor tomato can and he was a heavyweight or, at least, he was easily transformed into one.) Anyway, J.J. spent much of the flight with a pair of satin boxing trunks spread across his lap while he unravelled the threads along the waistband, inserted twenty thin cylindrical lead weights, each weighing a pound and a half, then sewed the waistband back up again. Fortunately the weights made the waistband of the trunks tight, which held them up.

When J.J. and his fighter went to the gym to workout and meet the officials, the officials looked askance at the fighter. "He has dense bones and heavy flesh," J.J. assured them.

And the day before the fight, the middleweight from Vancouver weighed in at 191 pounds.

He lost the fight but he didn't care. Neither did J.J.

Once I ran into J.J. on the street.

"What you got going?" he asked.

"I'm invited to a party tonight, and it's required that I bring a date. But I don't have anybody to bring."

"What kind of people are going to be there?"

"I don't know, really. Some musicians and probably some rich people, given the street address."

"Hey, I'll be your date."

So we went to the party in Shaughnessy. The first thing I thought when we walked in was how these people were going to react to him. Yet from the moment they laid eyes on J.J., they treated him like some visitor from a land they'd never dreamed existed. They were polite but slightly incredulous.

My clearest memory of that evening is of J.J. sitting on the white leather sofa with people all around him hanging on his every word—"It talks!" One story was about the time he was arrested in Wyoming due to some fight card that didn't live up to the expectations of the townsfolk.

"I got sentenced to thirty days. The first day, I noticed the deputy swept up at two in the afternoon. It was August and very hot, the door open to catch any hint of a breeze; he'd just sweep the dirt out that open door. Same thing the next day. I was the only one locked up. So when he wasn't sweeping or doing paper work, the deputy would pace, sit at his desk, get up again. I started chatting him up. Third and fourth day, he swept at two in the afternoon. Finally, I said, 'Look, I'm even more bored than you are. Why don't you let me sweep up?'"

The deputy let J.J. sweep up but kept a close eye on him. He let him do it the next day but kept less of an eye on him. By the third day, the deputy was relaxed enough to let the friendly convict sweep while he snoozed. When he woke up, he found J.J. back in his cell.

But on fourth afternoon, when he woke from his snooze, J.J. was gone. "I went out the door along with the dirt. I ran down to the freight yards and caught the first train leaving."

One of the men at the party wasn't going to be fooled by any tall tale and exclaimed, "You expect us to believe a story like that?"

J.J. smiled, took out his wallet and displayed a newspaper clipping: "Jailbird Swept Away While Deputy Dozes."

TAKE 108

LIST WRITTEN IN BLUE INK WITH BALLPOINT PEN ON A PAGE OF LINED PAPER TORN FROM A 4" X 6" NOTEBOOK

At the behest of musician and music producer Amy Andersen, I made a list of my favourite vocal recordings. I did this while living in Saigon for seven months in 2004. Amy was going to produce a CD of poetry, songs and music. I'd write the poetry and songs, and she would compose the music. It never came off; neither did one that was going to be produced by a foundation in Vietnam. In the latter case, the lyrics didn't get past the censors. I believe Amy wanted the list in order to try and understand my orientation, which would help her in writing the music. I think it was to be a top-ten list—there is a space between 10 and 11, and 10 is Cliff Edwards, who I would have saved for last (the best for)—but I just carried on:

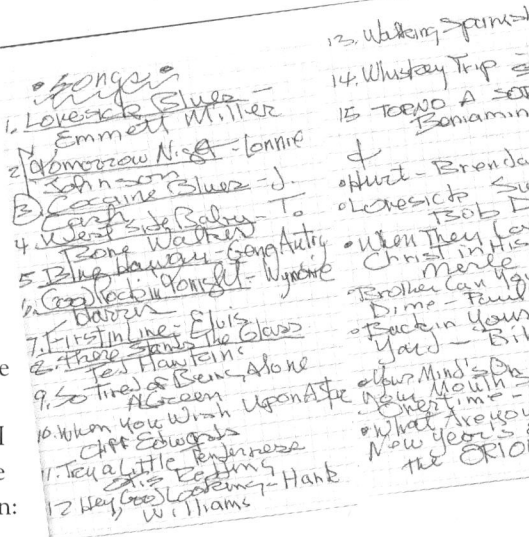

1. "Lovesick Blues"—Emmett Miller
2. "Cocaine Blues"—Johnny Cash
3. "Tomorrow Night"—Lonnie Johnson
4. "West Side Baby"—T-Bone Walker
5. "Blue Hawaii"—Gene Autry
6. "Good Rockin' Tonight"—Wynonie Harris
7. "First in Line"—Elvis Presley
8. "There Stands the Glass"—Ted Hawkins
9. "Tired of Being Alone"—Al Green
10. "When You Wish upon a Star"—Cliff Edwards
11. "Try a Little Tenderness"—Otis Redding
12. "Hey, Good Looking"—Hank Williams
13. "Walking Spanish"—Tom Waits
14. "Whiskey Trip"—Gary Stewart
15. "Torna a Surriento"—Beniamino Gigli
16. "Hurt"—Brenda Lee
17. "Lovesick Subterranean Blues"—Bob Dylan
18. "When They Laid Jesus Christ in His Grave"—Merle Haggard
19. "Brother Can You Spare a Dime"—Paul Robeson
20. "Back in Your Own Backyard"—Billie Holiday
21. "Your Mind Is on Vacation (but Your Mouth Is Working Overtime)"—Mose Allison
22. "What Are You Doing New Year's Eve"—doo wop version; can't recall the singer—Ravens?

Looking at this list now, maybe ten years after making it, I am surprised to find that I'm okay with it. I would, however, add Peggy Lee's version of "I'll Be Seeing You," an absolutely devastating work. Perhaps I'd replace "First in Line" with the great Elvis's "I Was the One."

(IMAGE EDIT: had to re-do this one, no idea where the hell it went!)

TAKE 109

FRAGMENT TORN FROM THE UPPER LEFT-HAND CORNER OF AN ENVELOPE: CONTAINS THE RETURN ADDRESS OF CHRISTINA KIROUAC OF WINNIPEG, MANITOBA

I was at the Winnipeg International Writers Festival with a small literary biography I'd written called *The Long Slow Death of Jack Kerouac*. A young woman came up to me, said she was a niece of Jack Kerouac, and spelled her name the original way. She told me that everyone whom she'd ever met in the Kirouac family was ashamed of the famous writer and that her father had warned her against even reading his books.

Christina was a professional boxer and performance artist. "I have a few billboards around town," she said, and described them. I saw one on my way to the airport. There was an attractive blond woman pictured, naked up top, but her breasts were covered by red boxing gloves; one could just see the waistband of red-and-white satin boxing trunks. Blazoned across the billboard was that old line from a joke that had been current when her uncle was a young man: "My girl can't wrestle, but you should see her box."

I never did ask her what her father thought of that.

TAKE 110

20" X 20" MAP FOLDED IN QUARTERS, LABELLED "CATTLE COUNTRY OF PETER FRENCH"

The letters are on a background that represents a cow skin; surrounding the legend are symbols of different cattle-company brands. Two-thirds of the map shows the south-central part of Oregon and the route of French's 1872 cattle drive to California. The cattle were driven from French's ranch at Frenchglen on the Donner und Blitzen River, south of Burns, and in a southwesterly direction, skirting the northwest border of Nevada and entering California near Fort Bidwell. The other third of the map traces the route down through the Paradise Valley, then west near Susanville to the Sacramento River and finishing up at San Jacinto.

French, who was born in Missouri, accompanied his parents out west in the early 1860s. His folks settled near Colusa, California, and his father started a sheep ranch. Young French found the work boring and got hooked up with a Dr. Glen, who owned a large ranch. The doctor employed him as a horse breaker and later promoted him to foreman.

The two men got along very well, and Glen hired French to head up into Oregon to reconnoiter the territory. There near the Steens Mountain, French set up the P Ranch that eventually encompassed nearly 200,000 acres. In 1872, he and his men drove cattle from the P Ranch to Dr. Glen's place in California. Glen was shot and killed by an employee in 1876. The next year, French and his men survived an attack by Paiute Indians, but French was shot and killed the following year by a neighbour over a boundary dispute.

Somewhere around 1990, I went with Joe Ferone, a good friend and a jack-of-all trades, down to the ranch country south of Burns in the Steens Mountain. He was to take photographs, and I was going to write an article for a travel magazine produced by one of Canada's big newspapers. They were doing a special essay on the United States and asked me to come up with an unusual idea, an article that would describe a relatively unknown area of a state or would show a

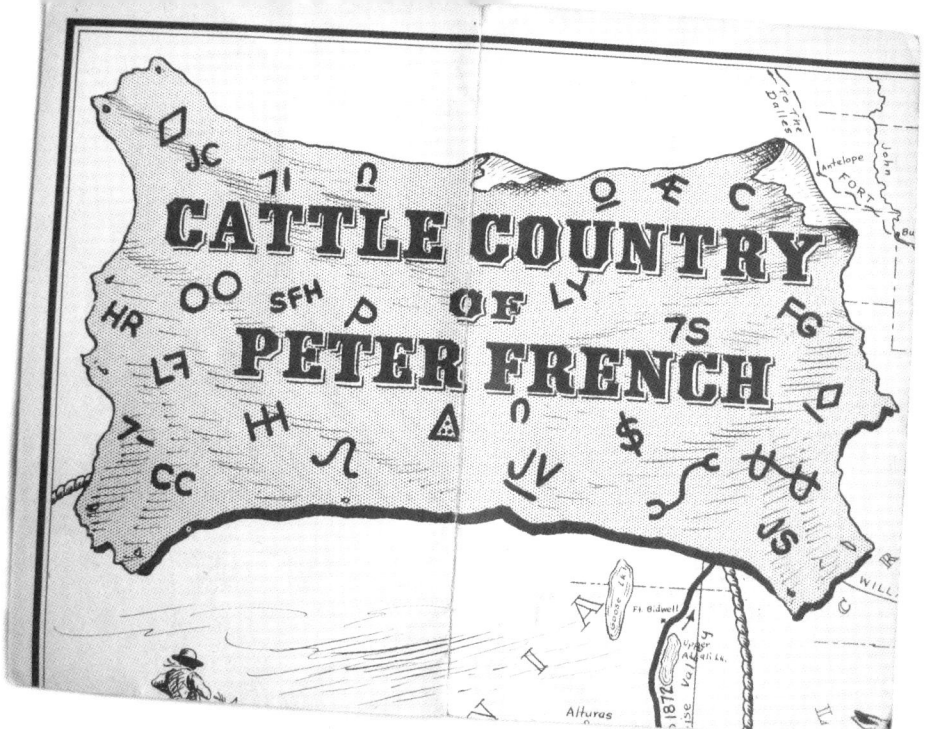

state in an unexpected way. I told them I wanted to do New Jersey: Unknown New Jersey. They laughed, but I would have gone into the considerable—relatively speaking—wilderness and discussed the peculiar history and people of the pine barrens. The editor laughed. He thought I was fooling him. The desert country of Oregon was my second choice.

Joe and I went down there, hooked up with a young rancher and spent a couple of days roaming around on horseback near Barton Lake. On the way out of the high desert, we stopped at the top of a ravine for a look at the moonscape country. There was a husky, balding man by the top of a cliff looking down. He was wearing a T-shirt, chinos and boots, and looked familiar. He appeared to be sad and deep in thought, so we did not disturb him. I told Joe I thought it was Ken Kesey, who was from those parts. The next day, I read in the newspaper that Kesey's son had just died.

TAKE 111

YELLOW, 4" X 8" INVITATION TO ATTEND THREE EXHIBITIONS AT THE ART GALLERY OF THE SOUTH OKANAGAN IN PENTICTON, B.C. (THE PLEASURE OF YOUR COMPANY IS REQUESTED ......) ON 2 APRIL 1993, A FRIDAY, AT 7PM

My show was one of the three. Jack Davis's exhibition, called *Lighten Up*, was in one gallery; Frances Hatfield's *Recent Drawings* was in another room; my show was called *The Sunnyside of the Death House*.

The Gallery of the South Okanagan is a beautiful spot on the lake, I had a good time and they paid me. That reception was also the first time I ever read poetry in public. The gallery director, Brenda Fredrick, had approached me, saying, "I hear you're a writer, too." I allowed as how I was. She told me that Mr. Davis had asked her several times if he could read his poetry to the guests. Ms. Fredrick wasn't opposed to the notion but thought a single reader wasn't enough to make an event. So she asked me to read. I had published my first book of poetry, *Palatine Cat*, in 1978, so here I was getting my first opportunity to read in public. I did read, and got another invite five years later when my second book of poetry, bearing the same title as my art show in Penticton, was published. Carol Ann Sokoloff, musician and wife of Richard Olafson, publisher of Ekstasis Editions, told her husband that she thought the poetry was musical and that it might be nice to have me read in front of her band. This happened in Victoria, the winter of 1998.

TAKE 112

CHROME-PLATED WOODEN BOX, 2" HIGH, 3" WIDE AND 6" INCHES LONG, THAT HOLDS A RAZOR AND ACCESSORIES MANUFACTURED BY THE WILKINSON SWORD COMPANY OF ENGLAND

The inside of the box is lined with blue satin and contains, besides the razor, a leather strop folded into a metal clasp, three blades and a small tube of "anti-corrosive strop dressing."

There are also two booklets, three by six inches, folded in thirds that give instructions for using the razor. Interestingly, to sharpen the blade, the strop must be threaded through the head of the razor assembly.

I bought this box at a second-hand store in Ottawa, not long after moving to Canada in the fall of 1968. I have been carrying it around ever since. I used it once shortly after purchase. The razor set is the "Three-day Model." There is a grooved wooden tray to hold the two unused blades that are still coated with the anti-corrosive strop dressing.

I believe the set dates to 1935, though it bears a close resemblance to a model Wilkinson offered for sale in 1909.

I have always liked the look of it, the attention to detail in its manufacture, and the weight of it. If you bought something like this when it was new, you held onto it; it was solid and important.

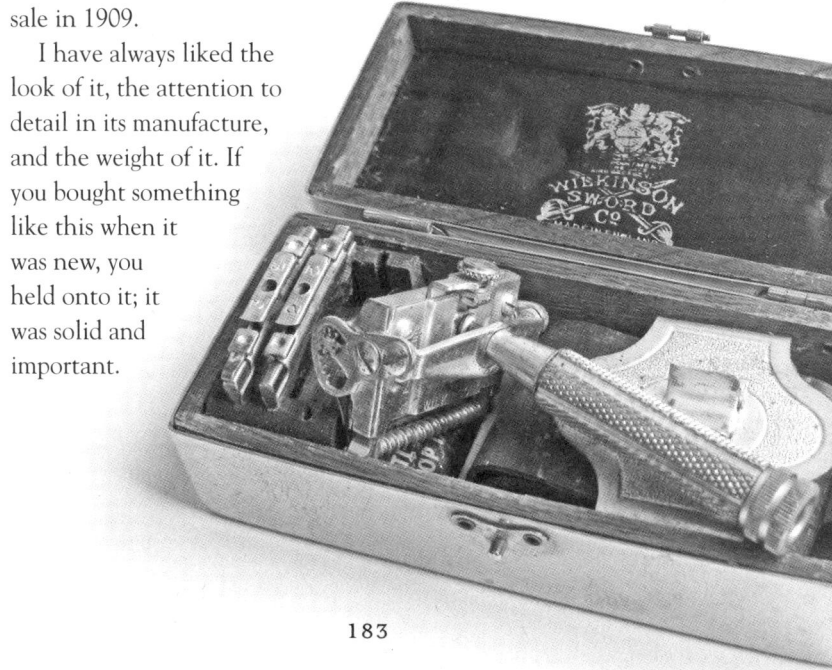

TAKE 113

COLOURFUL GUATEMALAN ZIPPERED POUCH; 6" X 5", SEWN WITH GREEN, BLUE, RED, ORANGE, YELLOW, PURPLE, BLACK AND WHITE THREAD

Probably bought in Antigua. Filled with various items. First out is a receipt for entering Nek Chand's Rock Garden at Chandigarh in the Punjab, in 2009. This work, covering twenty acres, may be the greatest individual artistic achievement of the 20th century.

That statement will not sound grandiose to anyone who has been to the gardens. Nek Chand, still alive at ninety-four as I write, was a clerk in the planned city of Chandigarh. On his way home from work in the evening he bicycled past the town dump. After awhile, curious, Nek began to prowl the dump, and eventually he began collecting material—porcelain, wire, plastic, metal bits, cast-off jewelry. To save this stuff for future use, Nek Chand had to carry it through the jungle on the far side of the dump; it was also necessary for him to carry a lighted torch to keep away tigers. For years, he transported material, arranging it in separate piles. After deciding he had enough raw material, Nek Chand commenced to build statuary of people and animals; he situated them in areas connected by tiled walkways that he also built. Before long, he was adding terraces and walls and waterfalls.

He laboured for fifteen years alone before his work was discovered by government officials. Instead of bulldozing Nek Chand's tremendous achievement and arresting him for appropriating government land, officials, overwhelmed by the site, offered him assistants and automobiles. He took the assistants. Work goes on to this day. Unfortunately, the assistants and volunteers don't have his raw, unimpeded sense of creation, and the new areas seem rather tame and formalistic. Nevertheless, the original gardens are a spectacular achievement. Other famous examples of bizarrely personalized homes and gardens—the Watts Towers and Coral Castle in the United States, Le Palais Idéal and La Maison Picassiette in France, the Tarot Garden in Italy—as spectacular as they are, seem to diminish in comparison.

The Rock Gardens of Nek Chand have, for several years, been the largest tourist attraction in India, next to the Taj Mahal.

TAKE 114

BUSINESS CARD THAT READS "EXPERT POVERTY MANAGEMENT, A DIVISION OF STARVING ARTIST INK"

It is the card of photographer Alan Sirulnikoff of British Columbia, a man who went all over North America taking pictures of roadkill, which resulted in a series he called *Dead Ahead*. He did a beautiful series on medicinal plants and one called *Hidden Voices*, a collection of back-alley wall scribbles from around the world. All his work shows wit and imagination, as well as a quality all too rare in contemporary photography: compassion.

TAKE 115

4" X 5" PIECE OF PAPER TORN FROM LARGE SHEET

One side consists of what remains of an advertisement:

TOP OF
Ogle
O Bing

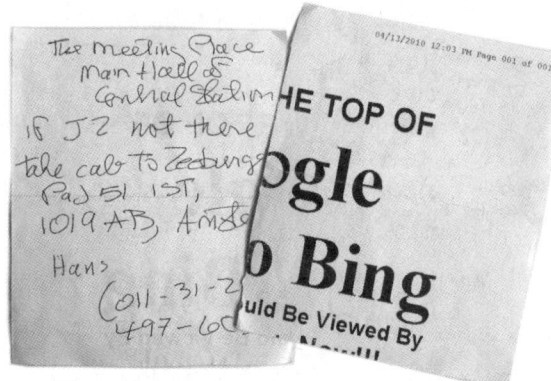

On the other side are directions written by me about what to do when I reach Amsterdam. I take the train from the airport to the central station and stand outside in the area known as the "meeting place." There I was to meet a man I had previously met only once, Jordan Zinovich.

    We were both invited to the Virugen (Fiery Tongues) poetry and music festival, which is held every year on Whitsunday weekend. Jordan knew Amsterdam well and showed me around town; despite my being jet-lagged, I remember we had a good time at a drinking club in an ancient riding academy. I've since come to know Jordan well, and we've seen each other again in Amsterdam, as well as in Manhattan and Toronto. He was born in Kimberley, B.C., and lives in Brooklyn. He's been all over the place, working as a shepherd in Greece and studying drums in West Africa. He's a damned good poet, too.

    "if JZ not there take cab to Zeeburger, Pad ___ etc. Amster."

TAKE 116

THE GREY CAP OFF AN OLD PLASTIC .35 MM. FILM CANISTER; A RED PLASTIC TOKEN SUCH AS IS BOUGHT FOR ALCOHOLIC BEVERAGES; A SMALL HOTEL/MOTEL SHAMPOO BOTTLE, LABELLED "LOTUS" WITH A LOTUS STEM AND BLOSSOM SPROUTING FROM THE TOP OF THE "S."

TAKE 117

NAPKIN ON WHICH, IN BLACK BALLPOINT-PEN INK, IS WRITTEN, BY ME, "MEALY BUGS ARE AN IMPORTANT FACTOR IN PINEAPPLE WILT"

This is something I always try to keep in mind.

TAKE 118

A SMALL PALE-GREEN AND CREAM BOX SUCH AS MIGHT HOLD THE DIAMOND BRACELET YOU'D BUY YOUR SPECIAL FRIEND

It's from "Morgan's." The box contains human teeth and parts of human teeth. The three intact teeth, molars, are very small. The teeth are only slightly discoloured. One has a large cavity. There are twenty-one fragments. Where these came from I have no idea.

Here and there, I have among my dearest possessions other teeth, most of them from animals, but some from humans. Please note that I do not obtain these teeth by nefarious or illegal methods! When people know you do assemblage-type art, they give you things they've found or don't want any more or that have popped out of their mouths. I'm serious.

In this way, I have collected everything from skulls to stained glass. I live in the country now and, thus, accumulate plenty of bones, teeth, antlers and skulls. Feel free to send along, care of the publisher, any similar items.

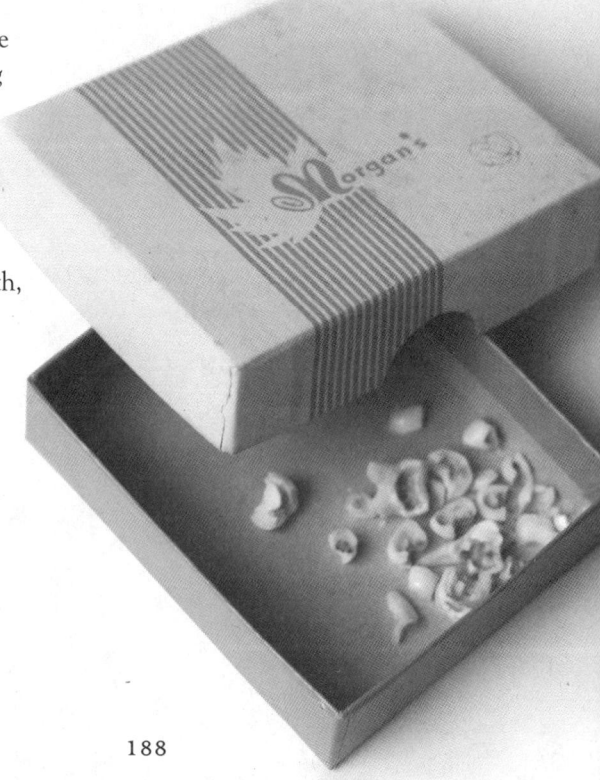

TAKE 119

ONE SEASHELL. A BRIGHT CUBAN PESO COIN. A RECEIPT FOR PURCHASE OF A BOOK COSTING $10 AT CITY BASEMENT BOOKS, ELIZABETH STREET, MELBOURNE, AUSTRALIA ON 08/11/2008.

Three objects that seem, at first, to be completely random and without meaning, and seem that way the second time, too. On the other hand, there is an entire world to be created around them. Maybe I found them on the beach at Guardalavaca. A woman from Melbourne had come across a second-hand book about treasure buried on a local beach by revolutionaries after looting a bank in Holguin. She disappeared; at her campsite these three items were all that remained, and I stumbled across them while walking along that beach with my new Norwegian friend Jan-Erik Lepsoe, and he recorded a song I wrote about it all that you hear on his CD *On the Country Side*.

TAKE 120

4" BY 6" COLOUR PHOTOGRAPH OF A CAR OWNED BY ME AND TAKEN AT GIBSONS, B.C.

It is highly decorated and perhaps recognizable as a 1978 Pontiac Acadian. It is decorated on a travel theme and festooned inside and out with metal cars, trucks, boats, motorcycles, helicopters, airplanes, globes of the world and memorabilia from locales around the world but—no cheating—only from places I had visited. As well, there are mascots and insignia—from other vehicles that acknowledge travel, travelling or geography; for instance, in this picture you can see "International," "Big Horn" and "Explorer."

The photograph was taken at a mid-stage of work, so the car became even more crowded later. It attracted so much attention that it often took me an hour to get home from the time I left the video store, five minutes away from my trailer. I entered the car in several "art car" shows. It was an immense pleasure to drive this car. I still own it, though I haven't seen it for over five years. It's locked in a small garage somewhere in British Columbia.

TAKE 121

RED PLASTIC COW WITH THE HEAD OF A ROOSTER. I KNEW I HAD ANOTHER OF THESE IN THIS SWEET ASSORTED BOX.

. . . . I live on a farm way out in the woods and wouldn't be surprised one of these days on one of my hikes to come across a cow with the head of a rooster, though I'd be more likely to come across a dzho which, as most people know, is half-cow, half-yak. I believe I had one of those in the Sweet Assorted box—I mean, a model of course—but it was stolen, probably by the same fool who pilfered the signed photograph of my first road buddy, Count Nicolai Navrotilini, known fondly as Count Garbage. That eight-by-ten glossy, turned sepia, was the item in the box of which I was most fond. The Count in full French Foreign Legion rig looking imperious and impish at the same time. But that, as Mr. Kipling said, is another story.

Jim Christy is a writer, artist, and tireless traveller. The author of more than twenty books, including poetry, short stories, novels, travel, and biography, his travels have taken him from the Yukon to the Amazon, Greenland to Cambodia. He has covered wars and exhibited his art internationally. Raised in inner city Philadelphia, he moved to Toronto when he was twenty-three years old and became a Canadian citizen at the first opportunity. His most recent books are the novel, *Nine O'Clock Gun* and the poetry title, *Marimba Forever*. A resident of British Columbia's Sunshine Coast for many years, he currently resides in the township of Stirling-Rawdon, Ontario.